CW00382574

Praise for *I See, M(*

"It made me feel nearly every emotion under the sun. Sad and hurting in places, angry in others but also happy and laughing, inspired and hopeful."

"The life story of a woman coming to terms with a very complicated childhood and finding herself as an adult"

" …. the way you described your relationship with food was incredible."

"You are honest and vulnerable and take responsibility for your mistakes and growth along the way."

"I cried for you, I cried for your mum and I cried for myself. That search for your own life and happy place is so strong in me and everyone I think."

".... a brilliantly raw and honest read."

"This is real life, in all its glorious and terrible moments."

"After reaching the end, I was left wanting more…"

"A story of growing up sensitive in a world that doesn't meet your needs."

I SEE, ME

Philippa's journey from
less than to *enough*

PHILIPPA ROBINSON

Copyright

© November 2021 Philippa Robinson
ISBN 978-1-3999-0933-4

Philippa Robinson has asserted her right under the Copyright, Designs and Patents Act 1988 to be identified as author of this book

All rights reserved. No part of this publication may be reproduced, stored in or introduced into a retrieval system, or transmitted in any form, or by any means (electronic, mechanical, photocopying, recording or otherwise) without the written permission of the author. Any person who does any unauthorised act in relation to this publication may be held liable to criminal prosecution and civil claims for damages.

For permissions contact Philippa Robinson via www.safeandsupported.co.uk.

Disclaimer

This book contains some material you might find disturbing. Examples include violence, neglect, alcoholism, death and disordered eating. Please do not read this book if any of those subjects may not be good for you right now.

This book has been written from my memory and, as we know, the human memory is deeply flawed. I have not knowingly changed details and I have written it to the best of my ability, from my perspective and from the memories I have about the specific events.

Poems

All the poems in this book are written by the author, Philippa Robinson.

This book is for Little Philippa, my inner child, who always knew I was in there and refused to let me die.

I am not what happened to me, I am what I choose to become

Carl Gustav Jung

PROLOGUE

THE YEAR IS 1969. Harold Wilson is the Prime Minister in the UK. Richard Nixon is the President of the United States of America, and in July American astronaut Neil Armstrong will become the first man to walk on the moon.

Decimalisation is still 2 years away, the Internet 14 years and mobile phones 16 years. It has only been 2 years since the passing of the Sexual Offences Act 1967 which legalised consensual homosexual acts in private in England and Wales between men aged 21 and over.

These events happened just over 50 years ago at the time of writing this book but, it seems like a century given the way things have changed since then.

THE DATE IS MONDAY 10TH FEBRUARY 1969. *Blackberry Way* by The Move is top of the charts and in a town in the north west of England I enter the world bang on my due date. Born under the sign of Aquarius, the first child born to my young parents. My Mum and Dad had to wait until my Dad turned 21 to get married, and 13 months later, I am here. My Mum is 21, and my Dad has just turned 22, the first of their friends to have children.

I am quite a novelty.

CHAPTER 1

I like to close my eyes. I find great comfort shutting out the visual world as it's a lot to take in at times. My nervous system is sensitive to stimulation and to shut off the view can be quite a relief. In the past there have been things I'd rather not see and this probably has something to do with it as well. When I close my eyes, the underside of my eyelids become a wrap-around screen and it's all I can see no matter which way I look. As I relax with my eyes shut and tune into the noises around me, the shapes appear and commence their gentle dance across the screen. First I see the birds, their tick-shaped, black bodies swooping gracefully around the milky sky of my mind. They twist and turn with ease, gradually slowing down until I blink and the dance starts again. I like watching them, seeing their grace and ease of movement, something I have longed to accomplish myself but never managed. I long to fly with them and be free.

After the birds come the water monster

(think Nessie) and the sky is transformed to the murky water of a loch. I'm not as keen on watching Nessie, more of a worry if I let myself dwell on it. These shapes are called floaters and they are, in fact, tiny fibres that clump together in the vitreous fluid in the eye as the fluid becomes more liquid as we age. I have had floaters for a long time so I am used to them. I recently discovered that floaters can be caused prematurely by hypersensitivity when the nervous system is overstimulated. I thought that was so interesting.

I also get this weird line across my eye sometimes, like a black and white spinning barrel going round and round in my eye. I can see above and below the spinning barrel but not through it and when this happens it feels like I am running fast on the barrel trying not to fall off, like the roller obstacles you see on *Ninja Warrior* on TV. Except I feel sick and disorientated instead of strong and powerful like a ninja warrior. This rolling effect usually lasts about half an hour and then goes away. It's the start of a migraine I believe (possibly a migraine aura but I've never had it diagnosed). It usually goes away and doesn't usually get any worse.

It's January 2017 and I find myself at the A&E department of Bristol Eye Hospital. The festive break had been the usual stress it often was in our house and it was a relief to be getting back into the work and school routine. On the second day back at work, I realised that a strange thing that had been going on with my right eye hadn't gone away. I am used to all sorts of strange things going on with my eyes as I am very short-sighted (to those of you this means anything to, I am -16 in both eyes!). It was like about two thirds of what I could usually see in my right eye was covered by a grey, cloudy smudge that I couldn't wipe away. It was irritating but I wasn't overly worried. A few people at work suggested I get it checked and as I had been too busy before Christmas to go for my annual sight test, I rang and made an appointment.

A week later, I walked up from work and arrived at the opticians but within 10 minutes I was on my way to the eye hospital A&E department trying not to be too frightened. My optician is fabulous; he is a clever, articulate, funny and kind man who I trust implicitly and when he took one look and said I had to go to the eye hospital, I knew something was up. He told me he thought he knew what was happening but didn't want to give me a misdiagnosis. I needed to get it checked at the eye hospital. Luckily, I live in Bristol and we have great facilities right on our doorstep, so after a 20-minute walk, I am at the eye hospital. I am incredibly nervous but I just walk, one foot in front of the other, trying not to think about it. I am good at ignoring my feelings so I sing to myself to distract my mind from thinking about what is happening. Even whilst I am singing to myself, I know I'm doing it as a distraction. This sort of defeats the object doesn't it? Knowingly distracting myself must mean I know I am worried about something which is why I am distracting myself. Whatever it is, I am a master of it and I just walk. I am holding myself together.

Bristol has had an eye hospital since 1810 and the current building was opened in 1986. It is an uninspiring, I would go as far as to say an ugly, red-brick building a short walk from the city centre. You walk in and immediately you're in a vast waiting area where everyone seems to look a bit confused and it is full of mainly older people. On any given day I am sure they have people of all ages through the door but every time I have been there it seems to be full of older people. Like eye problems disproportionately affect older people. It just goes to reinforce my weary feeling at the time that I am old and very tired.

The A&E waiting area is big but it feels closed in as there isn't much natural light at ground level and the fluorescent lights glare mercilessly down on the people patiently awaiting their fate. I go to the desk, give them my details and then I find a chair in the corner to sink into and wait. I am expecting to be there a while.

Surprisingly I am called through to see a nurse after about half an hour. I am silently pleased and think to myself I might be back at work by lunchtime. It seems like a sign that maybe things are going to be ok. The nurse asks me to read a letter chart and then puts some eye drops in my eye to dilate my pupils. Naturally our pupils open and close to allow the requisite amount of light into our eye. The drops force my pupil to open as big as it can and to stay there. It will help the doctor look at the back of my eye. The drops in my eye feel like someone is stabbing the sharp tines of a fork into my eyeball over and over again for about 20 seconds and then it eases. I am very grateful when it stops as I have just about managed to stop myself from crying. I am still holding it together.

I go back to the waiting area and wait. And wait. And wait. It's A&E for goodness sake, and I am very grateful to have a specialist eye A&E so close, but with my pupils dilated I can't read, I have a headache as everything is so bright and it's extremely boring. I am still holding it together, just.

After about 4 hours, I am called in to see the Registrar. He is around mid-30s, he looks like he has far too much to do (which he has, no doubt) and I sit down on a chair he points to while he bows his head to read my notes. Then, without saying much, he swings around in his chair to face me over a table-mounted contraption, that looks like it could be an instrument of torture. He tells me to sit up at my side of the instrument with my eye looking into a tube-like thing. He shines a very bright light into my eye (which is extremely uncomfortable when your pupils are forced open) and looks through whatever he has on his side of the machine. He's still not saying much. If I'm being picky, I'm not rating his patient manner 5 stars at this stage. It only takes a minute or two, then he sits back and tells me that what I have experienced is called a CNV, and the sight loss I am experiencing is permanent. I can't hold it together any longer.

At that moment, I am sitting in the same chair but everything around me has just stopped. Like this is a TV show and the viewer has pressed pause so they can go and make a cup of tea. If there had been a bird in the room, it would be just hanging in mid-flight, wings ready to flap. The only sound I can hear is my heart beating and it's so loud. "Boom, boom" all around me as if to announce the ominous arrival of a malevolent presence. Then a gulp starts in my low abdomen, creeps up to my mid abdomen and then races up, up, up until my shoulders lurch with the force by which it leaves my mouth. It is a cry like no cry I have ever experienced before or since. I sob uncontrollably for just a few seconds and then as quickly as it started it stops. I recover my composure, I apologise and I ask what it means.

From his chair, which seems a long way across the room, he looks sympathetic and he explains that CNV is Choroidal Neovascularisation which means I have a new blood vessel that has grown into the back of my eye and it is leaking fluid onto the retina. The damage that has been caused is permanent. The main thing now is to stop any further damage.

How has this happened?
What can be done?
What was it called again?
WHAT IS HAPPENING?!!

I am on my own at the hospital. This won't come as a surprise as you read my story and get to know me. I don't need anyone. I am a coper. I can do it on my own. All my life I have done things alone and it has almost been my life's work not to need anyone. My needs are for me to meet and me alone. I am totally devastated and very frightened - am I going to go blind? - but I recover my composure and leave the hospital with the promise of a clinic appointment for the following week to come in the post.

I am still feeling woozy from the eye drops and the hours of waiting and as I walk out of the main door I am struck by how bright it is outside. A wall of light smacks me in the face and it's all I can do to keep moving forwards. It is not very sunny but with my pupil dilated, January is pouring into my eye and the only way I can stop it is by closing my eyes. I have a bit of a wobble and put my hand on the wall to recover my balance. I am aware I must look a bit strange but try to focus on moving. I take a deep breath or two and start moving my feet. Then it dawns on me, where am I going? Shall I phone someone, shall I walk to work, what should I do? Oh, I know it is nearly 3pm and if I walk to the boys' school, I can catch up with Mark, my husband, picking our two boys up from primary school at 3.15 pm. That's it, that's what I'll do. I have a plan. Off I go!

I shuffle along feeling sorry for myself, looking at people as I pass and realising I can't see their heads if I look straight at them. To see their faces, I have to look at them from the side which makes me look like a salty old seadog scrunching up my mouth and cocking my head to say "Aha me hearty". *Quite comical really but I'm not feeling the fun of it just now.* For days I have been telling myself it's nothing to worry about and somehow, now the reality is worse than I could have contemplated, my sight seems even worse than it was that morning. I am trying not to think about it, but I am scared. I don't usually get scared and I don't like it.

I arrive at the school, where I see Mark's car parked waiting for the gates to open. He gets out as he sees me coming and I fall into his arms and sob on his shoulder. I didn't even tell him I was going to the eye hospital; he thinks I'm back at work after my optician appointment. He's surprised to see me at school and has no idea what to think about me crying. He asks me gently what the matter is, and I tell him "I've lost a lot of the sight in my right eye, and it's permanent". "Shit." Yes, it is shit, and I cry again.

Moments later my optician calls me to find

out how I got on at the eye hospital. He gets noticeably angry when I tell him that I was told the damage is permanent. He doesn't say they're wrong but he gives me the distinct impression that maybe there is some hope.

As I finish my call, Mark arrives with the boys and we set off home. It has been such an exhausting day all I want to do is go to sleep but there is tea to cook, washing to do and the dog to feed. Come on Philippa, pull yourself together.

CHAPTER 2

When the "eye thing" happened, I was 47, living in Bristol (I am a northerner by birth, but I have lived here since 2001), happily married (well, you know how it is - not every day is happy but we do pretty well I think) to a great man and we have lovely boys aged 8 and 9 and a rescue terrier called Bob. I have a great job in a law firm that I enjoy. We don't live an extravagant lifestyle and we have enough money to enjoy ourselves and do most things we want to, within reason. On the face of it, I am living 'the good life' and have nothing to worry about. In fact, someone said to me a couple of years later when I was telling them what had happened, that they thought I was living the perfect life. The true picture was very different.

Things hadn't been good between Mark and me for a couple of years or so. I was angry a lot of the time and when I wasn't feeling angry I felt alone and unhappy. Mark and I were having some pretty awful rows, and I was seriously wondering if we were going to make it. Initially I put it down to having 2 small children, quite close together in age, and no help. It was just me and Mark and it was intense. There was never any let up. We both worked but I had gone back part-time so I had more time with the boys. I was also doing everything in my power to bring my boys up with kindness, tolerance and patience as I was adamant they wouldn't have the upbringing I had. With hindsight I was trying too hard but I had no parenting role model to follow, just one I desperately didn't want to follow. We made it up as we went along and it was really me making decisions, taking the lead and I came to resent the responsibility that I had taken upon myself. On the outside, we looked like one happy family loving life, but inside I was dying and I didn't know why. I thought there must be something wrong with me to seemingly have it all and still be so unhappy. There was a deep ache of dissatisfaction that I couldn't shake off no matter how hard I tried to reframe it and be positive.

There were times Mark and I would row and it felt like a sort of out-of-body experience. One minute I was shouting at Mark, letting him know in no uncertain terms how I felt about something he had said or done, or more likely something he hadn't said or done, and then next thing it is like I have floated out of my body and I am standing at my side watching my hands flail around as I embellish my words and listening to the vile things coming out of my mouth. I was truly horrible and as I listened I couldn't believe I was actually saying those things. I was stunned, mystified, and yet I couldn't stop it and I would watch as the scene continued to unfold in front of me. It never ended well but we would reach a point of exhaustion and slink away to our respective corners to lick our wounds.

There was one weekend we were supposed to be going away, but we had a row on the Friday morning and I told Mark to take the boys on his own so he could see what it was like without me. We were in trouble. Whatever "It" was, it was eating me up from the inside.

Partially losing my sight made me even more desperate. I had spent my life making sure I needed no-one, and whilst I had a family that I loved, I knew I could manage on my own if

Mark and I split up. I believed the only one I could rely on was me. How was I going to manage, though, if I couldn't see properly or, worse still, if I went blind? Something bad was happening to my right eye; what if it happened to the left? Then I would be totally useless, and what would I do then? I had spent my life being useful, helping people, organising, doing things. I believed that that is why people wanted me around, because I was useful. Who would want me around if I was useless?

WHAT THE FUCK AM I GOING TO DO?

This is what was going round and round in my head, and it made me increasingly desperate. Inside, whilst I had been gradually dying, there was also a volcano raging. The fire in my core was getting hotter and hotter and I was going to blow. About a week after my first trip to the eye hospital, I went to a clinic appointment where they basically did nothing. I was supposed to be having a dye test to work out where the fluid was coming from but they decided they already knew the answer to that, so instead a treatment plan was needed. I appreciate now, with the benefit of hindsight, that they needed to see me in clinic to work out what to do but my desperation for clarity meant I felt nothing but frustration. Frustration piled on top of my need to be useful which in turn was covering my buried fear of being unworthy of love was too much - that volcano erupted. The pain and anguish flowed out of me in a torrent of rage aimed at my husband and children, probably for something trivial. It went on and on until I fell to the floor in what was probably an act of surrender. I knew I had to find some help. I told my husband, and I truly felt it, that if I didn't get help, I would have to leave as I was destroying everything that mattered to me, my family, and I was worried I would screw the boys up. I was in serious trouble and I decided to look for a counsellor.

About 4 weeks before the "eye thing" happened, one of my brothers had recommended a book to me by Melody Beattie called *Codependent No More*. Reading that book started me on a path of no return. At 47, I finally realised I couldn't deny any longer the effect that my childhood had had on me, and more to the point still was having.

Codependency is complex and the simplest

way I have found to explain it is that it is our responses and reactions to people around us. In my case it meant my reaction to my Mum's drinking and her reaction to my reaction. Like I said, it's complex. It is this complexity that means alcoholism and other addictive behaviours are family illnesses, not just an illness for the addict.

Reading the book made me aware of my codependent relationship and when I started looking online for a counsellor, I thought a good place to start was to look for one that worked with codependency. There was only one I found in my area that mentioned codependency on their profile and I called the number and left a message. I have no idea what message I left, but it would have been something garbled about needing help with codependency and can she help me.

Later that evening, she called back. I was in the middle of trying to get the boys to put their pyjamas on, and I wasn't in the mood to speak on the phone but I was curious enough to answer the phone as it wasn't a number I recognised. When I realised it was the counsellor calling me back, I changed almost instantly, from the parent trying to cope to the lost soul who needed help. We arranged to have an initial meeting the following Tuesday to see if we were the right fit for each other. As I ended the call, I realised I'd done it now; I was going to have to go through with it. I was going to get some help.

I met with the counsellor and, to be honest, I didn't warm to her but I knew I needed help and she was an expert as far as I was concerned. I was relieved when she said she could work with me; it felt like I passed the first test. I arranged to see her the week after for my first proper session. It's funny because now I usually recommend that people meet a few counsellors to find the right fit but I didn't call any others, let alone meet any. I just wanted help and she was there and available. Looking back, I think I was trusting my intuition that she was going to be the right counsellor for me.

My first proper session was at 10.45am on the following Tuesday morning. I didn't work on Tuesdays so I took any time she had available that day. I dropped the boys at school, went home to put some washing on and then ended up almost being late as I faffed around too much at home. I guess I was putting it off as long as possible. I was desperate to start doing the work, as I badly wanted to shift the dark cloud around me, but at the same time the prospect of what might lie ahead, when I had no idea what that might actually be, really scared me.

The counsellor had been very clear that I was to wait outside until my start time and not to ring the bell early. She was, and still is no doubt, very good at setting boundaries. She seemed very bossy at first but I was clear on the extent of the container she created for me and the work I was doing and I felt safe there. It was important for me to feel safe.

My first session was difficult. I was closed, not keen to be real, but I knew I needed help. I suppose I was looking for an easy fix. She did well to eke an initial commitment of six weeks out of me. I suppose I thought that might be enough. I think I knew that might be all I could cope with. I don't remember many details of that first session. I know that I cried and told her how wretched I was feeling. I do remember that I came away with two lasting memories. One was her telling me, after I'd told her some details from my childhood, that what I experienced wasn't ok and it wasn't what anyone could call a "normal" childhood. I had told myself all my life until then that what I experienced wasn't actually that bad, it wasn't like I'd been abused or anything. There were a few instances of physical violence over the years and they were enough to add to the feeling of being unsafe but I wouldn't have called them abuse.

What I hadn't taken into account was the persistent absence of a caregiver to pay attention to my needs and wants, who was there for me, to talk to me, care for me, nurture me. They were physically present but emotionally absent. I was expected to deal not only with my own feelings, mainly to suppress them so they didn't cause anyone else any problems, but also to deal with their emotions too. It was a lot for a child to take on. It was, in fact, emotional neglect. It was a shock to understand that I had been neglected. I was shocked and comforted at the same time. To hear that it wasn't normal was a relief and a huge leap in my understanding.

The other thing that I remember from that session was that she congratulated me on not being a substance addict. She would later discover that my addictions were less obvious but at the end of that session, to know that someone independent had heard some of my story and told me it wasn't ok, and that I had done well to survive as well as I had, made me feel better in myself than I had done for a long time. She told me change takes work but change can happen. She gave me hope.

In the first few sessions we concentrated on the present and my feeling of being unable to carry on. All that went through my mind at that stage was "there must be more to life than this". She helped me see that doing everything for everyone else and putting myself at the bottom of the pile was taking its toll, and we started to look at why I didn't think I deserved better.

Gosh, that was hard. All my life, I had not thought I deserved much just for being me. I worked hard, I looked after others, I was helpful and kind, and because I did all that, maybe I deserved some kindness; but to think that I may deserve that just for being me never figured, ever. It was a real shock to me to discover that others believe they are worthy in their own right; there is a lot of research that shows that those people who we see as worthy of love, kindness and respect usually believe they are worthy of it. So, on the flip side, those that don't believe, don't get it. One has to believe one is worthy to receive. That blew me away.

She asked me what I would like to do for myself if I could. I can't tell you how hard it was to think about that, not because I wouldn't be allowed to or anything like that but it was just an alien concept to want something for myself. At that time, every couple of months or so, my friend and I would go for a long walk at the weekend, 8-10 miles and somewhere away from the city. That was such a treat. If I could, I took the dog so Mark wasn't left with the dog and the boys but Bob the dog is unreliable around livestock, so I didn't always take him. What else did I want to do? I couldn't think. I started slowly with maybe an hour in the coffee shop with a book. I also spent a few hours helping a friend clear her garden. Sounds strange perhaps but I find clearing a mess up quite satisfying. My friend was grateful as her garden was wildly overgrown, but she did me a favour letting me help - doing something physical, with good company and achieving a visible result is something I will always enjoy. It's as though witnessing the removal of clutter with my eyes enables my mind to sort its own stuff out too.

The more I tried to think about little things I could do for myself to make me feel more satisfied, the more I realised this wasn't what I was missing. It was a start though and it was slowly making a difference. I was learning that by taking time for myself, life didn't stop, the world didn't collapse and no-one told me I couldn't do it or resented me for doing it. In fact, I was a teeny bit happier which was better all round for everyone.

It was my birthday not long after starting counselling and I bought myself a lovely silver necklace with a solid, heart-shaped pendant. My husband wanted to buy it for me, but I wanted to buy it for myself; it symbolised my commitment to myself, to believing I deserved better, and that I deserved some love. It is still my go-to piece of jewellery that I wear when I'm feeling vulnerable or need a confidence boost. Such a small thing but especially important.

A few weeks later, I met a friend who was 4 years into a psychotherapy course. We had talked before about her course, and she had tried to persuade me to do a counselling course – she thinks I'd make a great counsellor. How funny that idea seems now, knowing what I've been through to just get to some basic level of understanding about myself. She talked about the foundation course where she was studying – an initial year-long course that can then lead to a counselling or a psychotherapy qualification. I liked the sound of it and she kept telling me that as I was already having therapy, I'd done the hard bit. I was looking for something different to my day job, I just didn't know what. I thought about the course on and off for a week or so and, without much in-depth consideration, found myself completing the application form, then at the interview day, then being offered a place and then paying my money to start the course in September. I had no idea what I was letting myself in for, but something drove me to sign up. The funny thing is I really did think starting therapy was the hard bit.

Whilst I was waiting for my course to start in September, I was making good progress with my therapy. I was working hard at my job and feeling a bit better in myself. It must have been hard for Mark as I was changing, wanting more for myself, which did feel inherently selfish at times but ultimately I knew it was what I needed. I knew that there had to be more to my life than feeling like I had to serve everyone else. I was still very closed in therapy and not admitting things to myself, let alone feeling able to say them out loud to my counsellor. I felt judged, not because she made me feel like she was judging me, but because ultimately I was my own harshest critic, and I found myself deficient on all levels. I am good at telling other people to be kind to themselves but awful at applying that advice to myself.

On the interview day for the foundation course back in April, I had gone thinking I would feel like I didn't fit in. It was an alien environment to me, and whilst I have spent my life fitting in, I was always careful to pick a role I thought I had a good chance of fitting into. I had no real confidence to try something out of my comfort zone. So I was on the interview day looking at all these people (all women bar one) and thinking I didn't fit in – most of them were working or had worked in a support or care environment, and I was a lawyer. The lady who interviewed me said, "we don't get many lawyers here". Maybe that was part of the attraction – desperately seeking something new. I was offered a place and on the 19th of September 2017 I took my first steps into the Bath Centre for Psychotherapy and Counselling (BCPC) in Bath.

I looked around the room at the 18 of us, 16 women and 2 men. All a bit nervous, no doubt, and trying hard not to show it. My usual way in new situations is to make eye contact with a friendly looking person or two, smile and crack a joke, usually self-deprecating. On this occasion I didn't get the chance as we were all sitting dutifully and quietly when the tutors came in. Two ladies; one shorter with a round smiley face and hair cut in a short, wavy bob, the other taller, athletic looking with long, straight, blond hair and a much sterner look on her face. One of these women would play a pivotal role in what was to come for me. The ice-breaker to open the day was "tell us your name and a little bit about how you are connected to your name".

CHAPTER 3

Philippa – Greek origin meaning "lover of horses"

My Mum told me that she called me Philippa because she went to school with a girl of that name who had long blonde hair, was tall and athletic. Things I think my Mum would have liked to be, but she was 5'4"-ish, big boobs and not that willowy. When my Mum told me that story she seemed to say it with an air of wistfulness and I always thought that meant I'd been a disappointment. Perhaps she was wistful that she didn't turn out like that herself, but growing up I had a very deep, pervasive sense that I was a disappointment.

I was the oldest of 4 with 3 brothers. One brother was 20 months younger than me and the other 2 were 10 and 13 years younger. There were often comments from my Mum that she liked boys better than girls. I found that hard to hear. She was an only child and went to a convent boarding school, so had been surrounded by girls. Maybe that's where she learned not to like girls; I don't know. Maybe she didn't mean me when she said boys were better than girls but it felt like she meant me too.

In my early teens when she was shouting at me for something (she shouted a lot so it could have been anything), she yelled at me that she regretted having children so young as it ruined her life (she was 21 when she had me). After the initial shock of hearing that, and after a few days brooding, I took that to mean that I, just by being born, actually ruined her life rather than it being anything about her decision to get married and have children to get away from living at home with her parents. It's what made sense to my young brain. As Julia Roberts says in *Pretty Woman*, "The bad stuff is easier to believe".

I now know that, in order to make sense of a traumatic experience, our minds make up a story to protect us and it is safer for a child to think they are the problem than to think their primary caregiver isn't capable of taking responsibility for their own decisions. If they aren't capable of that responsibility, then it might not be safe to be in their care and that is not a story our minds want to dwell on. On the other hand, if it was my fault, then I could work on myself and that was a safer story to believe.

It was difficult to feel that I was to blame for Mum's obvious unhappiness. I say obvious but if I was asked to explain how I knew she was unhappy I'd struggle to put it into words. It wasn't that she actually said "I am unhappy", it was the seriously bad temper, the sighs, the general discontent with anything and everything. People on the outside mainly saw the sunny side of her but that's not the side I saw most of the time. The comment that having children so young had ruined her life had stuck with me and that certainty that I was to blame was part of the reason why I tried to be a "good girl" all the time and a "people pleaser" but no amount of being good or trying to please ever made a difference. So I tried harder and as it continually failed to work any magic on the situation, the guilt just multiplied.

One day, when I was about 12 or 13, a thought occurred to me that maybe she was pregnant with me, and had to get married, and that is why it was my fault. If she hadn't been pregnant, if I didn't exist, then she wouldn't have been so unhappy. It was a terrible thought to carry around with me and it festered for a few weeks, intensifying as I brooded on this disturbing inquiry. I decided that if I could find out when my Mum and Dad got married I'd be able to work out if she was pregnant. Great idea, only problem was I couldn't just ask her. She was married to my Step-Dad by now and my Dad was never mentioned. Never. She would most likely be cross with me for asking, and by cross I mean anything from dismissive annoyance to full blown rage and I wouldn't know which one I'd get until it was happening. She was mean when she was angry and I spent all my time trying not to make her mad so I wasn't going to poke that bear (think grizzly not teddy). I thought about it a lot and then one day I was alone in the house which was a rare occurrence; I'd usually have at least one brother if not more left at home with me.

Our house at that time was an old telephone exchange converted into a house so it was a weird shape. You walked into the big L shaped kitchen and then straight in front of you was a glass door into the windowless hall. The hall then led to the other rooms. In the hall there was an old desk, I think it's called a bureau, and you pull down the front, pull out two support arms at hip level on each side to rest the front on as a writing surface and then inside there are all sorts of drawers, recesses, nooks and crannies. There was a lot of stuff in there and it's where important papers and things were kept. I figured that if I was going to find out when she married my Dad, the answer would be in there. The thing was I didn't have long and if I got caught I would be in so much trouble. My desire to know was strong enough to do it anyway but I was terrified of what would happen if I got caught.

With my heart hammering, a massive knot in my stomach and fear pounding in my head I opened up the desk. It was a muddle inside, it always was, but more of a mess as I think my Mum had been looking for something. Just my luck. It made it even harder as I would have to leave it looking messy like it was when I found it. I carefully looked through the papers, envelopes and all sorts of stuff. There was even the plait of my hair from when I had insisted on having it cut short a few months before. She hated my short hair and I didn't know she'd kept my plait. Funny. I remember being surprised she'd kept it and thinking "why did she keep my plait when she doesn't even really like me?".

It seemed to take ages for me to sift my way through the papers and always having one eye on the back door and my ears pricked for the car coming back slowed me down. The hall was pretty dark as it didn't have a window so I needed to have the light on to see but if they came back they would be able to see me immediately as I'd be illuminated by the light. It was madness but I just needed to know how long it was after they married that I was born. Finally, I found some papers in an old envelope. In my desperation to open the envelope I held it upside down and the contents fell on the floor. "Oh no" I said out loud to myself but handily it had separated the papers and I found a long legal document (what I now know was an affidavit which is a sworn document submitted to the Court to support one party's position in a case) that quite near the beginning clearly stated that they had married in January 1968, the year before I was born. 13 months! Thank god for that.

The relief was worth the effort to find it but quickly that turned to fear again in case I got caught so I set about replacing everything as best I could to hopefully look like it did when I started. I finished before they got back and had a little while to sit with my new found information.

It was such a relief to realise that their wedding hadn't been my fault after all. I had no idea quite how fucked up that was, as if it could have been my fault anyway. That was just normal to me. I was relieved to find out I wasn't the reason she got married but it did nothing to relieve the weight of feeling unwanted, unloved and as a consequence a deep feeling that I was unlovable.

To deal with my feelings of worthlessness and the worry that if I didn't prove myself, I might not be able to stay, I turned into the ultimate "people pleaser". I was the first one up in the mornings from about age 10, cleaning dog mess up from all over the kitchen floor (no-one ever mastered house-training the dogs), making cups of tea and coffee and taking them to my Mum and Step-Dad and then getting myself off to school. When I got home from school, Mum would go off and ride her horse, leaving me to feed the younger kids and my oldest brother to sort out the stable. People used to laugh that we were the nanny and the groom. Seriously, people used to laugh. What about our childhoods? What about what we needed or even wanted? I felt we were lucky to have a roof over our heads, so we kept our heads down and got on with it. I genuinely felt that I had to be useful to stay; my place in that house always felt fragile.

My original nickname was Cacklecan (because I talked so much) but it was against this background of fragility that when my nickname changed to Porky I just accepted it. I was about 13 or 14 at this stage. All the boys in the house (3 brothers and Step-Dad) thought it was hilarious to call me Porky. They'd shout it to me when other people were in earshot. There's a picture of me on a trip to London where I had to stand under a sign for a café called "Porky's". The look on my face says it all. I was a source of ridicule for everyone and I hated it. I was so intensely embarrassed that my own family thought so little of me that they thought it was all right to do that.

Nicknames are one thing, but Porky is up there with some of the worst I've heard. Maybe someone more robust than me could have coped with it, and I probably gave the impression that I just brushed it off, but inside I was crying. Looking back, I must have had enough spirit that I wasn't going to be broken, and I wasn't going to show them how much it hurt. It wasn't the sort of family I could ask them not to do it, as it would have made them do it even more. There were times I could weather it but the worst thing about it was it added to my already growing feeling of worthlessness.

I tried harder and harder to please. My Mum's friends would marvel at how helpful I was, how lucky she was to have me, and all she could say was I created my own problems for her. To this day, I don't know what those problems were. I wasn't rebellious at all; I toed the line, I did everything asked of me, and more. I did well at school. Maybe I was too good? Ironic isn't it that in search for love and kindness from her I got yet more rejection and I think, underneath it, she wasn't happy with the situation either.

CHAPTER 4

I think I was a daddy's girl. Over the years I have heard things like "dads and daughters have a special relationship" and I have often wondered if I was special to my Dad. I think I was but part of me wonders if I like to think that because I didn't feel special to anyone else. I have very few memories of the time I lived with my Dad and we were a family and I used to put that down to being so young. It was only when I had children of my own and I realised they have memories from being quite young that I understood I must be blocking my own memories out for some reason. It is a way of disassociating myself from that part of my life probably because it's too painful to remember. I feel sorry for that little girl who had her world ripped apart and at such a formative stage.

I recall a time when I was about 4 and we were upstairs. The stairs had 3 steps down, then a quarter turn to another 10 or so steps, then another quarter turn to the last 3 steps down to the ground. The carpet was red and the banister was fully boxed-in and painted white. It was a bit like a tunnel when you're too small to see over the banister with the house wall on one side and the solid, boxed-in banister on the other. The only open bit was at the bottom of the long run of stairs; instead of a wall there was a run of thick bamboo canes from the ceiling down to the stairs. It was the 70s! I have no idea what happened but my Mum was angry. No idea if it was with me, probably was, but she certainly took it out on me. I recall the rage, the big red face looming in mine. I don't recall the words but I remember the spittle landing on my face as she yelled. I remember her grabbing a handful of my long, blonde hair, yanking me towards her but next thing I was falling down the stairs. I was frightened but not too much as I didn't really get what was going on. I fell down the first 3 stairs and bumped hard into the wall at the bottom before the momentum made me turn and bump down the flight of 10 steps. Bump, bang, one step at a time each one creating a deafening noise in my head. I rolled over at one point and ended up feet first, going at some speed as I hit the bottom of that run and then to my surprise I broke through the bamboo canes and hit the floor below with a mighty bump. I just lay there stunned. There was no movement at the top of the stairs for a few seconds before my Dad came running down and scooped me up in his arms. I started to cry as the shock of what had happened jolted me back to the present moment.

My Dad was kissing my face and making soothing noises, asking if I was ok. My Mum was nowhere to be seen. I don't remember what happened next but I was in one piece, nothing broken and I think my Mum and Dad were just bloody grateful. I do remember that my Mum was annoyed about the broken canes and I was left feeling that it was my fault. I have very few childhood memories, especially of that first house we lived in with my Dad, but I have never forgotten that incident. My Dad was like a knight in shining armour to me that day and he stayed on that pedestal for a very long time.

My Mum and Dad split up when I was about 7

and that's a stage in a child's life when they are becoming aware of the world around them (i.e. others rather than just themselves). They become sensitive to the feelings of others. It can be a confusing time and, whilst I can't imagine there is ever a better time in a child's life for their parents to split up, I can only imagine that my parents splitting up at that time made it even more confusing for me. Now I understand that I was a sensitive child, it makes sense to me that I would have felt the emotions of this time pretty strongly.

My Dad wore thick-rimmed, dark-framed glasses and used to wrinkle his nose up to stop them falling down. He was a solid trunk of a man, tall and widening out at the shoulders like a magnificent tree with blue eyes and blonde hair as his crowning glory. Think Viking. I remember him as always having a smile on his face. Whether that is because it is true, because he is smiling in the few pictures I have of him, or because it's what I want to remember I'm not sure. It's a nice memory so I'm keeping it.

The house where I lived with my Mum, my Dad and my brother had a single storey extension at the back that only recently I learned my Dad built. We used it as a playroom. It filled me with a warm fuzzy feeling, even at my advanced age, to now discover he built us that playroom himself. Across the back of the house, there was a bit of flat garden and then a steep-ish slope down to a lower part. It wasn't very big but it was a great garden to slide down on trays when it snowed. Bundled up in warm clothes, I'd set my tray down at the top of the slope and try to sit on it before it slid off downwards leaving me behind. If I did manage to sit on the tray, my Dad would gently push me and I'd usually fall off half way down giggling uncontrollably. In the summer my Dad would fill up the paddling pool and put the end of our slide into it so my brother and I could whoosh down into the cool water that would cover us from head to foot. We also had one of those garden sprinklers that was a bar with holes that rotated from left to right making magical arcs of cool water to run through. I have an overwhelming feeling of joy when I think about those times in the garden with my Dad.

Right at the bottom of the garden there were some shrubs and a fabulous tree that had amazing pink blossom in the spring. Cherry blossom I presume. I still love the spring blossom. I used to plant seeds and things with my Dad down there, hoping to watch them grow. It was our special place as my Mum wasn't interested. She preferred to spend time making the garden at the front of the house look nice, probably as that's the bit most people saw. I would love time with my Dad digging, finding worms and generally getting dirty. My Mum would be annoyed when I got dirty as she would rather I wore pretty dresses and stayed clean. Nothing she could do would make me want to wear those pretty dresses she bought and any pictures I have of me as a child wearing a dress are accompanied with a sour look on my face. I'd wear the dress if I had to but I wouldn't smile for the camera!

We had lots of animals. A rescue afghan hound, called Remo. Afghan hounds were pretty cool in the 70s. He was beautiful but nervous as he had been mistreated by his previous owner, a man, which meant he had a habit of biting men he didn't know. My Mum would make this hideous celery flan and we'd feed it to Remo who would throw it up outside. Mum used to think he'd been eating grass.

Good dog! We also had a cat called Tiger who I used to think of as my cat. He was a tabby, full of character. We went to pick him up from a farm and I held him in the back of my Dad's Triumph Stag car on the way home. My legs were ripped to shreds. We had two budgies and one day we came home and Tiger had somehow opened the cage and killed the bird that got out. We buried the budgie in a shoe box in the garden. We also had guinea pigs – we started off with two and soon ended up with more than we bargained for!

I think my Mum preferred animals to people most of the time and that says a lot about her state of mind. She was as uncomfortable with people as she was a performer so the more uncomfortable she felt the more she performed and boy could she put on a performance. It made her a great host and good company but not so great a parent. I feel disloyal saying this but it's true at least from my perspective. Time is a healer and I have much more awareness now but during my childhood it was hard.

My parents liked to throw parties in that house and on many a New Year's Eve me and my brother would be put to bed in my room as his room was tiny and his bed was used for the pile of coats! My bedroom was opposite the bathroom and I'd spend all night listening for people coming upstairs, opening my door by mistake and through the dark I'd shout "Bathroom is the opposite door". Occasionally my Mum would come up and get me to dance downstairs – for some reason she thought it was amusing for me to dance to *Tiger Feet* (by Mud), the dance where you have your hands on your waist and you twist this way then that, shoulders in and out. All very tame but the point is I was brought out as some sort of show piece, the entertainment. I used to hate it but of course I didn't dare refuse. A small part of me liked being asked to do it because it seemed like I was appreciated in that moment. Appreciated for what? Putting my embarrassment to one side in favour of doing what my Mum wanted? The thing worse than being embarrassed was being ignored which would have been the outcome if I refused to do my performing monkey tricks. I doubt any of it was done with real malevolence but just because no harm was meant didn't mean no harm was caused.

When my parents split up, although we saw Dad for a few years (3 or 4 years I think) it became less and less during that time. There was often an atmosphere after each visit and then eventually we just didn't go anymore. The split wasn't mentioned at all, life just went on and once we had stopped seeing him he never got mentioned. It was like he had never existed, as if his part in our lives had been erased, and with that I was left for many years with questions about what happened, why did it happen, was it my fault?

As things deteriorated between my Mum and my Dad, and after we hadn't seen him for quite a few months, the Family Liaison Officer from the Court visited one day. I knew they were coming as my Mum had told me they were going to ask whether I wanted to carry on seeing my Dad. I can't recall if Mum actually told me what to say; I definitely had the feeling that I should say I didn't want to see him but I can't remember how I came to that feeling. I was probably about 11 at the most and although I was mature for my age I was in no place to understand the ramifications of a decision like that. I remember being surprised that anyone was actually asking me what I wanted as I had never been asked before but I also knew I didn't have the option of saying what I really wanted.

The rows leading up to that day had been fierce and every time me and my brother went to see my Dad there would be a heated exchange between my Mum and my Dad or my Step-Dad and my Dad or all three of them whilst my brother and I waited in the car. At that age I had no idea what was happening but what I did know was that every time we saw my Dad it caused problems at home. So whether I was coached to tell the Court Liaison Officer that I didn't want to see my Dad or whether I felt it from what was going around me, that is what I told her when I sat down in a big armchair opposite her in our very chintzy, flowery, 80s over-the-top lounge that day

I remember her being a kind looking lady but very official with a clipboard and she was scribbling away, writing notes. We weren't usually allowed in the lounge unless it was a special occasion so I knew this was important. As she spoke to me it felt unreal. How ludicrous was it that I was being asked if I wanted to see my Dad? I wanted to scream that yes of course I wanted to see him but I knew I couldn't do that. I was too frightened of how angry my Mum would be. I didn't think I was allowed to have what I wanted if it meant trouble for everyone else. I knew my place and it was right at the bottom of the pecking order. I sat there calmly, the picture of a well behaved child and said I thought it would be better if I didn't see him. I don't think I actually said that I didn't want to see him rather that I thought it was better, but no-one ever questioned who it would be better for. I think I was hoping she would twig that it wasn't the truth, that she would save the day.

I was deemed old enough to be asked such an important question but I was far too young to appreciate the repercussions; the sense of the betrayal I would feel for the next 20 years, the part it would play in my life over the years to come and ultimately be part of my recovery after my breakdown in 2017.

I said what I said to please my Mum and Step-Dad and to make life easier for us all at home. I knew I was betraying what I wanted but I did it because I felt I had no option. It seemed selfish to get what I wanted if everyone else would suffer as a result. What I didn't know was that what I wanted should have mattered as well.

Living with my Dad was never an option in my mind. I think that was because I felt he'd left me and my brother and I thought he didn't want us to live with him. I didn't feel wanted by my Mum and I didn't feel that my Dad wanted me either. I felt like such an inconvenience. My Dad was lovely, kind, good fun; not volatile and dismissive like my Mum. I longed to live with families that I read about in books or with the families of my friends who always seemed so nice and happy. Much as I felt Mum didn't want me I knew she didn't want my Dad to have me and with her powerful father and lawyer husband on her side, my Dad didn't stand a chance. He told me as much later on. He truly thought he was doing the right thing so it must have been pretty dire for him if he believed his kids were better off without him. How wrong can you be?

I'm not naive enough to think that life with Dad around would have been rosy. Or that would have meant I wouldn't have endured the things that came with my new family; to constantly be at the bottom of the pile, to be the skivvy to clean up after everyone, to look after the babies, to feel like I didn't matter, to be ridiculed over my size, to feel the shame that came from the ridicule, to feel that I didn't belong, to not be understood, to be the "good girl" and the "people pleaser". But I do feel having my Dad around would have given me roots, something solid to grow from and some respite from the life I lived. I have a fantasy that it would have been a place for me to be accepted just as I was, to know I was enough just as I was. My Dad leaving cast me afloat with no rudder, I was adrift with a mother that didn't want me around, didn't even like me and I felt utterly alone most of the time.

The Fabulous Tree

*I look out of my bedroom window, what can
I see?
I see houses and gardens and hear children
playing, who can they be?
I see a giant lollipop that makes me smile
A big brown stick with a green top that lasts
a long while
In spring the top grows pink blobs that look
ever so sweet
The sort of thing I'd like to have as a nice
treat
In the winter the lollipop loses its top and
looks a bit sad
But it comes back again in spring and then I
feel glad
Daddy and me like to be in the garden
together
We plant seeds and grow things whatever
the weather
When I think of that place now, how I long
to be
With my Dad looking at that most
marvellous, fabulous tree.*

CHAPTER 5

Growing up, our home life, our family, that is our normal. I didn't really notice any difference between our home and other children's houses until I was in my teens. I suppose I didn't spend enough time in other houses to really see, and the time I did spend there, it was an utter relief to be out of my house. In my teens that changed as my friends had more freedom to do their own thing after school and at the weekend but I had to help out at home. I resented not being able to do things with my friends and if I was allowed to it was usually on the condition that I had one of my little brothers with me.

Like the time I wanted to go into town with my friend. I was about 13 and Mum said I could go if I took my 3-year-old brother with me. We went on the bus and he was great until he got bored and decided to leave the clothes shop we were in and go somewhere more interesting. When we realised we couldn't find him we were both distraught and had no idea what to do. We ran up the street to where my friend's mum worked and she got in touch with the shop we'd lost him in and someone found him coming back to look for us. He'd been to Toys R Us! Once I'd calmed down I was petrified about what my Mum would say but in fact she was ok about it. Probably because my friend was there too. The duality of that situation - playing second mum but not being mature enough to cope when it went wrong - is still a lot to get my head round sometimes.

I often felt that my Mum found life as a stay-home mum with 4 kids unfulfilling. In my 20s, I was struggling with my career choice and didn't know what to do, and her only comment was "I don't know why you didn't just get married and stay at home", so maybe it was partly her choice. She always said that she wasn't encouraged to work. She didn't do particularly well at school; she was a bit of a handful by all accounts. She would bunk off from school in Southport and somehow get to Liverpool to see The Beatles playing at The Cavern. She was once caught on the convent school roof where she'd climbed to write her name for posterity. I loved hearing her stories on the odd occasion she told us about her childhood. She did start nurse training but didn't like it much and jumped at the chance to pack it in when my Grandpa gave her a house for her 21st birthday present after she was married. As you do! My Dad worked in the family print business and I presume earned enough to keep us, so Mum didn't work. It was the 70s and some mums worked; some didn't. I think my Mum was bored and hadn't grown up with the belief that she had something to offer outside the home, so she didn't try.

School was my haven when I was younger. School and books. Oh, and *Come Dancing* on TV when it was hosted by Angela Rippon and Terry Wogan. I loved those fabulous, sparkly dresses and elegant dancers. I'm sure that's why I now love *Strictly Come Dancing*.

I read anything and everything. As a young girl, I loved the Nancy Drew and Hardy Boys mystery stories as well as the Enid Blyton Tales of the Twins at St Clare's and Mallory Towers. Books allowed me to escape into another world. Either the plucky Nancy who searched for clues and always found out who did it. Or the gorgeous Hardy Boys who went everywhere together solving crimes and saving the day. In some stories Nancy Drew worked with the Hardy Boys; what a dream team. The books were American and as such were great escapism but not attainable for me. The Mallory Towers books were my favourite, stories from an English all-girls boarding school where the camaraderie of midnight feasts, reading under the covers at night with a torch and whispered conversations after lights out were the norm. The idea of a splendid castle-like school on a cliff top overlooking the sea in Cornwall made my heart ache to be there. It was so far removed from my actual existence that it was like a fairytale. The main character started the first year getting into trouble but she settled down and triumphed in her studies and in sport. God I wanted to be like her.

I longed to go to boarding school. To get away. I would probably have hated it, to be honest, but my Mum hated boarding school so she was never going to send me. She did make me do an entrance exam for a private school that I passed, but I hated the school so much I got myself out of there after a term and back to the state middle school I would have gone to anyway. My Mum had to grovel to the headmaster after telling him her daughter was going to a school much better than his. Subtlety wasn't one of her strong points!

At the private school I stuck out as the newbie and I found it hard to make friends. I also felt I had gone from being one of the clever ones to average and I found that hard. When all around me at home was chaos and I had no idea how to navigate it, school was the one place I felt I knew the rules and I could do it. So to go to a new school where I was plunged into the unknown knocked the little bit of confidence I had. Thinking about it now, it might just have been a different setting and way of teaching and I may well have sussed it out but I just couldn't bear it.

Once I'd got out of there and was at middle school, I was much happier. I made friends with a girl who lived quite close to me and we travelled to school and back again on the bus together. I loved the freedom and having a real friend all of my own. On the way home from school we would walk to the bus stop with a boy we both liked and stand chatting with him at the bus stop for ages, letting bus after bus go by until one of us had to go. Happy days. We are still friends today, 40 years later.

In the last year of that school I was school captain and one of the 4 house head girls at high school. I was a proper girly swot and I loved school. There, people were kind to me. I found friendships hard, and I always found myself in an odd-numbered group, so if we had to pair up, I was always the odd one out. When we went to high school, another girl who lived near us joined me and the bus-stop friend on the bus to school but they got on the bus one stop before me and sat together. I felt pushed out and didn't deal with it well. I was devastated but didn't let it show and instead I sulked and hid my hurt behind a veil of indifference. The friendship with the bus-stop friend fizzled out and we didn't speak for about 3 years. By the time we left for university we were friends again and have been ever since. That situation of being in a 3 and feeling the odd one out would be a pattern I would repeat over and over again in life.

I loved school because I could do it. I was academic, I worked hard and it felt safe. When it came to my A-levels, I had a lovely maths teacher called Mr Sparks and he told me he thought I could do further maths (which was pure and applied, or mechanics by another name) even though everyone else who was doing it was doing A-level physics and I didn't do O-level physics. He told me he'd give me extra lessons if I needed help. He believed in me. So I did it, I didn't need extra lessons, and I did well. I have remembered Mr. Sparks and his kindness all this time.

I applied to do law at Birmingham University and got in. My Mum was so disappointed! She apparently, and unknown to me, wanted me to do vet science even though I didn't do sciences. Imagine being gutted that your child was doing law at university. That was my normal! It might have been because my Step-Dad was a solicitor – one useless lawyer in the family is enough, she said – and I didn't knowingly want to follow in his footsteps, but having a lawyer in the house made law more of a reality, I suppose. I didn't want to do maths so law seemed like an option even though at that stage I never intended to be a lawyer. I hated my law degree. It was a lot of theory, reading papers, writing essays. I hated it and was awful at it. They went hand in hand, I suppose.

For someone who had excelled at school, I even passed my driving test the first time, it was a shock to fail my first year exams at university and have to redo them at the end of the summer. I scraped through my law degree with a 2:2, but I made a great lawyer. I was practical, efficient, could work quickly with attention to detail and I was good with the clients. They don't teach you any of that on a law degree. I think a lot of degrees are like that – not so much like the job they lead to – so if you're finding your degree hard, take heart that work after university is a different thing altogether.

I don't remember when I realised my Mum drank a lot and that it was a problem. She used to like sunbathing and when she was still married to my Dad she'd get up a ladder with her friend and a bottle of wine or two onto the garage flat roof and pull the ladder up behind her. My brother and I were left to amuse ourselves. It may have been for short lengths of time, but I think it is more likely it was for longer. The length of time doesn't really matter. It was the impression it left on me; that we weren't wanted around. At that time, I don't remember lots of wine bottles in the house and my Dad said she wasn't a big drinker, as far as he knew, when he was around. Certainly by the time I was 13 it was a problem and I suspect it steadily increased over time.

I came home from school one day in my early teens and I remember she was standing in the kitchen doing the ironing. She had a can of diet coke on the windowsill behind her and I leaned over and took a swig. It was a bit of coke with a lot of vodka. I winced but didn't say anything and she pretended she hadn't seen.

My Mum liked a party, and she liked to be the centre of attention and of course, that meant getting drunk. I used to dread any social occasion as it meant I spent the entire time on high alert, watching for her tipping from nice drunk to nasty drunk, keeping my little brothers entertained, so they didn't annoy her. Generally keeping everything going while she entertained her crowd. I was never asked to do any of those things, I don't suppose it was expected, but I felt it's what I had to do.

When I was 13, my youngest brother was christened and my Mum got my bus-stop friend drunk on champagne (I wouldn't drink), and I spent a good hour cleaning her sick out of my thick, brown shag-pile bedroom carpet. My friend and I laugh about that now, but it still reminds me of the anxiety that came with my Mum and social events.

The drinking gradually got worse over the years. At 18, I ran off to university and never looked back. I left my younger brothers, to whom I'd been a second mum, who were 5 and 8, to the mercy of my Mum. The drinking was getting worse, but I think not having me there meant she had to do more, so maybe it kept the drinking at bay for a bit longer. When I came home from university in the holidays, she'd deliberately move things around in the house, particularly the kitchen cupboards, so

I couldn't find anything. When she saw me struggling, she used to tell me that was the price I had to pay for not being there all the time. She went out of her way to let me know that life moved on without me. I remember feeling she must hate me at times like that. It got so bad that I stopped going home during the holidays. I once spent the Easter holidays totally on my own in my flat at university, and I was lonely, but it was worth it. Thinking about it now, that was probably the first step I took towards breaking away.

When you have an alcoholic parent, their highs are your highs, and their lows are your lows. Especially when it's the main caregiver. The rollercoaster is tough and I hung on for many years, slowly distancing myself going home just at Christmas and special occasions; but not often otherwise. It took until my early 30s to get to the point where I couldn't ride the rollercoaster anymore. There was no big row or anything but I just stopped keeping in touch. My Mum didn't phone me either and we didn't speak for about 5 years. Life was much easier without the late-night drunken calls, shouting abuse down the phone, coming home to rants on the answering machine. It was hard though not having any communication with her, as though she had died but hadn't and she was out there somewhere seemingly quite content living her life having nothing to do with me. Looking back, I don't think she was very happy, and of course, the drink numbed the pain.

I spent a lot of my life thinking that if I had been a better child, my Mum would have stopped drinking. Surely she knew how much it damaged the family and yet she continued. It never occurred to me that it might be because she had problems with her own self-esteem. It never occurred to me that if I thought she didn't love me enough to stop drinking, then she didn't love the other 3 enough either. It just fed my belief of worthlessness and I didn't have the skills to see the picture more clearly.

It was probably after a terrible weekend back home that I returned to London (where I was then living) in a real state, called in sick at work and desperately sought a counsellor who could see me that day. I was 24. I knocked on the door and felt such relief when a grey-haired, portly, very kind-looking woman opened the door. I stumbled in, sat down and basically cried for the best part of an hour. I must have done some talking as I left with two very valuable new ideas: (1) It wasn't my fault that my Mum drank and she wasn't my problem to fix and (2) As she was either hungover, getting drunk or drunk there was no mum to have a relationship with. So no matter how hard I tried to make things better, to make her happy, to fix things, it was never going to work because my Mum would carry on exactly as she was doing until she decided to stop herself. That fabulous woman did such a good thing that day.

It wasn't my fault!

I had always thought, in some way, it was my fault, that somehow I was responsible for her unhappiness. If only I was a better daughter. No, it wasn't my fault. Those words made things better for me for a couple of years which at least got me through my training contract and saw me qualify as a solicitor.

My Mum would often pick my youngest brother up from high school. Only recently I discovered that the teachers would watch as she drove away, all thinking she was drunk, but no-one did anything about it. They would watch what they suspected to be a drunk woman driving her child away from school and they did nothing. NOTHING! This happened on many occasions. I find it hard to understand why they didn't do anything except that perhaps they didn't want the hassle or she was a white, privileged, middle-class woman and they thought it better to turn a blind eye. It is a miracle that over all the years she drank, she never killed anyone.

My Mum's drinking meant she often drove when she'd had a drink. I think I was aware of it but it wasn't something that really figured on my radar until one day in December when I was about 15. My Mum always went to her father's company Christmas party and we went too as it was in the daytime. This particular year I had noticed that she was drinking quite a lot of wine so I was on extra high alert when we left the party and got in the car. The boys were in the back and I was in the passenger seat. She was in a good mood which was unusual. It was December and pitch black as it was about 5pm. We had been at the party since lunchtime. The car park was pretty deserted which is just as well as my Mum drove round it a few times trying to find the way out. Once out of the car park we were on the main road, a normal single lane each way road, lit and there was hardly any traffic around. My Mum wasn't saying much as I guess she was concentrating. I was watching her intently for signs of what might be about to happen and something made me look ahead just in time to see that we were on the wrong side of the road with a car coming towards us. It was quite a way away at this stage so I had time to gently say to her that she needed to move over. I leant over to pull the wheel in case she didn't respond and our joint effort moved the car back over to the left side of the road. I somehow knew not to shout or scream as it would have frightened the boys and could have made her angry. After a few stunned seconds of silence, she started to laugh. I didn't hear her do that very often and it was a lovely sound to hear. I knew, though, not to trust it as it probably wouldn't last. I laughed too as I knew that's what she wanted. She wanted me to make her feel better, so I did. We laughed and laughed and I made a joke, in a silly accent, about us not being in France so we had to stay on the left. She laughed even more at that and we drove the rest of the way home in an awkward, uneasy but sort of conspiratorial, joyous, guilt and angst filled bubble. We laughed about it many times over the years but I knew it wasn't funny.

CHAPTER 6

When we were little, my Grandpa (my Mum's father) would have a bonfire party at his house. I loved those parties. He would collect his garden rubbish and as the year went on we saw the pile getting bigger and bigger. We knew it was going to be a great fire come bonfire night.

Grandpa made a lot of money in property development in the 60s and he built his own house on the side of a hill. From the front it looked like an ordinary bungalow with a big tarmac drive and lots of trees and bushes up the hill from the front of the house. The back of the house looked very different. It had a big cellar area built into the hillside and then the upper part came out from the hill and was supported by brick pillars creating a den-like undercroft area the whole length of the house. He kept his tractor there for cutting the grass and I loved to sit on that tractor when we were playing down there.

At the back of the house the large garden ran down the hill with lots more trees and bushes. He was a keen gardener and there was always work to do, cutting things down and tidying things up; a lot of material for the bonfire. Bonfire night was one of the few occasions where we got together as a family without lots of other people there too. There might be an odd guest but it was a family party. It always felt much calmer than other parties and more relaxed. Being outside in the dark and staying up later than usual was a real treat. It was my favourite time of the year.

We would have jacket potatoes cooked in foil in the fire and Lancashire hotpot which is a simple dish of meat (lamb or beef usually), onions, potatoes and carrots sliced and layered and cooked in stock until it falls apart. We didn't have a crust on ours but I think a crust is the more traditional version. I loved it with a pile of pickled red cabbage or beetroot. I sometimes cook it for my family and the smell of it cooking and the taste still send me straight back to bonfire night. We'd also have homemade parkin which is a heavy, loaf cake made with black treacle. Another northern culinary delight. The other thing we had was homemade treacle toffee which took your fillings out sometimes. It tasted so good though, like it was burnt but it wasn't. A smoky, chewy piece of heaven. I would always sneak extra pieces into my pocket so Mum didn't see how much of it I actually ate. Sometimes I'd find the mangled mess in my pocket a few days later, covered in fluff and as I chewed it would cheer me up being reminded of the party.

We would have a few fireworks and be allowed to put sticks in the fire until they set alight and generally just mess around in the dark with fire and eat lots of nice food. I remember it with such fondness. Grandpa would hold court. He was a good host always making sure guests were fed and watered and he could hold an audience with his stories. I was just thankful he kept everyone entertained so I could do my own thing.

There was a gorgeous weeping willow tree in his garden and in the summer I liked to hide in the middle of it pretending no-one could see me. In the winter there were no leaves but the willowy branches were plentiful and even without leaves, in the dark I used to pretend no-one could see me. I suppose I liked the idea of being invisible, even then, because it gave me a bit of quiet and a break from feeling not good enough. If I couldn't be seen, I couldn't be judged.

The fireworks were my favourite. I loved the drama and the spectacle, the colours, the sparkle and the loud noises. It was as though someone was firing pink, green, blue, red, silver and gold glitter from a cannon into the sky and then as mysteriously as the spectacle appeared it would disappear leaving the bright lights seemingly embedded in the sky for a second or two longer. The bangs used to make me jump, every time, but the whoosh of a rocket and those intense seconds of waiting for the bang followed by the rain of amazing shapes of all colours kept me rooted to the spot in wonder. It was a piece of magic in what wasn't usually a very magical life.

One year when I was about 5 we had the bonfire party at our house (my Dad was still around at this stage) and it was a highly anticipated event for me. I loved bonfire night and the opportunity to bring all the magic of a bonfire party to our house was almost more than I could take. Bonfire night was usually just us four and my Grandpa and Gran (she died when I was 10 not long after my Mum married my Step-Dad) and it felt like it was a party for the kids, me and my brother, rather than it being for everyone else. It just felt super special to have it at ours for a change.

One minute I'm outside, the next I'm being dragged inside by my arm. I have no idea what I did or said wrong. My Mum marches me upstairs and at my bedroom door she pushes it open and shoves me hard onto the bed. On the other side of my bed is an old wooden desk that my Grandpa got from somewhere and my Mum painted orange and purple to match the curtains. Remember it was the 70s! The desk is from an office and it's a big desk. As my Mum shoves me I land on the bed, I bounce and I can see the desk looming towards me. I am heading towards the corner and there is nothing I can do about it. Whack! My head hits the desk with a real thud and the noise echoes inside my head. There isn't much of a gap between the bed and the desk and I fall back onto the bed. I am stunned into silence and I look at my Mum silently pleading for her to come over and make it better. She strides over, checks I'm not bleeding and walks out leaving the words "that'll teach you" trailing behind her. Teach me what? To think I am so worthless that

that's all I deserve? That I am not loved? That I am unlovable? She was right, that taught me. I lay on my bed, curled up on my side listening to them have a good time outside and feeling afraid and alone.

I was probably hard work for my Mum at times, and perhaps I was just too excited by the whole thing. Maybe I said something I shouldn't have said. I now know I was a sensitive child and as well as making episodes like this hard for me to comprehend, it may have triggered something for her as well. I think now, after recalling this story, the events of that bonfire night are where I started to believe that if I was too excited about something it ended in disaster so I learned to not look forward to things too much.

CHAPTER 7

My Grandpa was my Mum's father. He was a big man. Physically he was tall, broad shouldered and handsome so he made quite an entrance into a room. I always remember him with ice white hair that was combed back with Brylcreem, a big nose with a bump in it where he broke it when he was younger and he always looked smart, even when he was doing "dirty" jobs. When I was younger he always had a cigarette in his hand and there would be a big pile of boxes of Dunhill cigarettes in his kitchen, bought duty free on his exotic holidays to places like Hawaii and Spain. We rarely went abroad so anywhere outside the UK seemed exotic to me. Dunhill cigarettes came in red and gold boxes and even they looked exotic. He was a real commanding presence and people took notice. When I was little he always seemed like a giant. One friend of mine (the bus-stop girl) used to say he reminded her of Willy Wonka, the Gene Wilder version from our childhood. An interesting comparison – a dark and mysterious exterior, testing everyone out but with kindness at the core. Sounds about right.

He was born in India on Friday 13th in 1921 and he always said Friday 13th is a lucky day. His father was in the army, I think. They came back to the UK when he was still at school and after school he went into the Air Force and served during WW2. He married my Gran after the war and they only had one child, my Mum. He made a very good life for himself and his family in property development. My Mum told me she often used to feel in the way as my Grandpa and Gran had a very close relationship. I suppose sending her to boarding school didn't help. When she wasn't at school she spent a lot of time sitting in the back of the car going round Grandpa's property developments.

I never saw much real affection between my Grandpa and my Mum and it seemed obvious to me, even as a child, that he disapproved of some of her life choices. He was a generous man and he was kind at times. He wasn't warm and cuddly.

I never met my Grandpa's father and I only recall meeting his mother once. Her house was really dark, the curtains closed even though it was daytime. It was all very strange and I was left with the impression that she was a sort of witch. I think that was because there was a real air of mystery around her; we rarely saw her and even then it was only for a very short length of time. I remember her in a long flowing white nightgown (even though it was the afternoon) with white long hair pinned up and looking very dishevelled. She had pinched features and a hook nose not unlike Grandpa's. Her living room had thick red velvet curtains which were closed so barely any light came in and you could see the dust particles dancing in the bit of the light that forced its way in through a gap. I was very young so didn't understand anything about that situation which seems very odd even now to the adult me.

My Grandpa was the middle of 3 boys and he didn't see much of his brothers. There is a picture of him, his brothers, his Mum and their nanny with their elephant (I'm not joking!) in India in the late 1920s and they all look a bit …. I think "detached" is the best word I can use here.

My Grandpa used to say, often, that the only thing wrong with young people was that he wasn't one of them. It's interesting thinking about him saying that as my memory is not of him ever being particularly interested in us children but maybe he was in his own way. My Gran died when I was 10 and he remarried within a few months which caused a great rift with my Mum so I never got to know him properly as I got older. I was always aware of my Mum's feelings towards him, mainly resentment and hostility, but I now understand it was much more complicated than that, and it felt disloyal to her to be overly nice to him on the odd occasion we saw him. Such occasions would usually involve alcohol so I was always on high alert anyway.

When he used to say that about young people, I think it was mainly because he struggled with getting older. He was very charming but even as a child the charm felt somewhat contrived to me. I think these days we would say he lacked authenticity. That makes sense as his aim in life was to make lots of money, which he did, and I believe the driver for that was to show his family how good he was. I don't think he knew how to show love and I think he passed that onto my

Mum. Just smile and pretend everything is fine. So perhaps what I learned from my Grandpa and my Mum was more about how not to do things. To break that pattern of striving to show people how great your life is when it isn't.

When I found out in my 30s that my Grandpa had told my Dad if he stayed away he, my Grandpa, would make sure me and my brother were looked after, it was a real wave of mixed feelings that flooded my body. I felt sorry for my Dad that he had been made to feel so useless and unable to provide that he had bought the line that we would be better off without him. I was also angry that he'd bought that line because I thought it was an easy way out. I was sick to my stomach that my Grandpa would do something like that. That yet more people in my life had so little regard for my feelings and what might be right for me even if it didn't suit them. I was angry that all these people had made decisions about me but, to my mind, with no actual regard for me. It felt like it suited them to have my Dad out of the way, to not have me and my brother visiting him and his family, to pretend to the outside world we were one big happy family. A truly happy blended family before the idea of a blended family was actually a thing. What was seen from the outside was more important than what was best for the people on the inside.

The whole thing stinks, it really does and even today I get angry, and also sad, when I write about it. I can feel the bile rising in my stomach and that uneasy feeling making my skin crawl. It's as if my brother and I were pawns that were bought off my Dad and he just let it happen. I was so hurt and angry when I found out but in another way it made me feel better. He didn't just not care; he didn't walk away with no thought as to how we got on. He genuinely thought we were being looked after and were better off without him. He also told me that he called my Mum once a year or so to see how we were getting on. I never knew that. So he had kept in touch, sort of, but with her not us. I was abandoned, that is what it felt like, but to know that there was more to it than that gave me a little bit of comfort.

The compassion for my Dad came later once I began to understand how hard it was for him. I also have compassion for my Mum as she was stuck in the middle of a failed marriage, a rich and powerful father and a new husband who she wanted to please.

CHAPTER 8

My Grandma, my Dad's mum, was a kind, caring lady in my memory. She was a big lady, not fat but tall with big, bouncy, wavy hair and a long oval-shaped face. She was a formidable presence. She was always dressed smartly in a dress or a skirt. She had these warts on her face that I found absolutely fascinating. I would stare at them and touch them. I thought they were somehow magical and made her very special.

Her husband died young when I was little and all the time I knew her she had her father living with her so she could look after him. She had a very ordinary house but welcomed me and my brother with open arms and was ALWAYS pleased to see us. She cooked a lot and there was often a big pan on the cooker steaming a suet pudding. Spotted dick was my favourite, not just because it had a funny name. A big tin of Birds custard powder in the red, yellow and blue metal tin would be on the side ready to be used when the pudding was cooked. I was in awe of how the powder could turn into the sublime yellow blanket for the pudding just by adding milk and heating. Oh and her jam! Tangy blackcurrant deliciousness oozing out of a jam roly-poly.

Me and my brother often went to her house with our two cousins who were similar ages and I have such fond memories of playing in the garden with them. My brother once set his hair on fire from a garden bonfire and he had to have a big chunk of his fringe cut out.

My Grandma had all the pictures we drew for her stuck up in the kitchen, like they were precious works of art. She made us feel special and I felt so safe there. The later visits with my Dad would be at her house but once we stopped seeing my Dad we stopped seeing her too. It was devastating.

I have very few memories of being with my Grandma, it is more a feeling, a sense of warmth and safety that I remember. One memory I have is that in her bedroom she had this rather grand dressing table in her bay window. It was an antique gold colour, had the most beautiful ornate legs and on top there was a matching mirror in three hinged sections so when you sat on the stool you could see yourself to the front, right and left. I had never seen anything like it. The dressing table top was glass and on it she had a silver tray holding a silver 4-piece vanity set; 2 brushes, a comb and a hand-held mirror. The brushes sat with their bristles down on the tray and the backs were inlaid with delicate flowers embroidered on a white linen background held in place by a piece of glass set neatly into the silver surround. The mirror had the same backing and the long elegant handle was engraved with a vine reaching up to the embroidered flowers on the back. The comb had a handle of ornately twisted silver and it was heavy to hold. I loved that vanity set and it felt like it held some sort of magical energy. Perhaps it was the energy of the lovely ladies who had owned it before Grandma, or even of my Grandma.

I wasn't allowed to play with it but every now and again if I was in her bedroom with her she would let me hold it. She would sit on the stool and gently pull me onto her lap and she would pick the pieces up, let me hold them for a minute and then put them back. We would do this with all 4 and with each piece she would tell me to be careful. They felt very precious in my little hands. Sometimes I felt drawn to it and I would pretend I was going to the toilet but instead I would sneak in just to touch it. I wouldn't pick any of the pieces up for fear of dropping them but I would just gently touch. That was enough. I preferred to hold them when I was safely sat on Grandma's lap but if she didn't have time a little touch was better than nothing. I have no idea what happened to that vanity set when she died but I hope it is being treasured.

When the Family Liaison Officer asked if I wanted to see my Dad anymore I didn't connect the dots to realise that would mean not seeing her either. My Dad did the best he could but he was fighting his own battles and wasn't able to fight my demons with me but Grandma was a force to be reckoned with and if she'd stayed in my life longer I feel things might have been different. When I was 14 or so she died of breast cancer and we hadn't seen her for about 4 years. My Dad later told me he was so angry that my Mum took us to the funeral (we sat at the back) when she hadn't let us see Grandma for so long. At that funeral I didn't even recognise my Dad, I thought he was my Auntie's new husband who I hadn't met yet. My Dad was in such a state he didn't see us and even if he had he wouldn't have been able to take it in. It still makes my stomach churn thinking about how physically close I got to him that day but I didn't realise.

CHAPTER 9

As a child I think I had an innate sense of when things weren't right and that seemed to be a lot of the time. I lived pretty much on high alert for things going wrong. To try and find out what was going on I became very good at eaves-dropping. I would sit somewhere in earshot very quietly, or usually I'd squat for a quicker getaway but if I was there for a while I would have to kneel as my legs got tired. My Mum would go mad if she caught me listening in. Now I know I am highly sensitive, it helps explain how I felt things so much and I also think the early trauma had deeply affected me. I didn't feel safe and I needed to know enough to protect myself as best as I could. It was survival.

One of my few memories from the first house we lived in, a real memory not one from a photo, was of my Mum on the phone one night not long after my Dad had left, practically begging the man on the other end (who would become our Step-Dad) to come over that evening. I was kneeling on the upstairs landing, leaning against the banister, and my Mum was on the phone downstairs. I must have heard her on the phone to make me get out of bed to listen. It was clear from what I heard that he didn't want to come over as me and my brother were there. From the way my Mum was talking, it left my young mind with no doubt that she'd rather we weren't there that night.

Perhaps she was lonely and just wanted some company and I misinterpreted what was being said but I definitely believed in that moment that we were an inconvenience. I think there and then I realised that as children of our Dad, we were going to be in the way of any new relationship and we had better watch out. I think that was the moment my "people pleasing", "good girl" tendencies began to form, in a bid to be allowed to stay I suppose. It was definitely a survival strategy as I truly believed we could somehow be sent away, I had no idea where to, but it was where the seeds of danger and lack of safety were sown.

One thing I did do wrong was I ate and when I ate I needed bigger clothes, and that was a problem. I would binge on anything I could get my hands on. So my Mum stopped buying the food I wanted to eat. To be honest, I'd eat most things as long as I could get enough of it to fill the hole. I seem to remember this started at the first house we lived in as I have a vague memory of standing in front of the fridge at night, lit by the light inside. If I could have got in and closed the door, I would have done. I ate because I was unhappy, lonely, sad. I didn't eat because I was hungry. I hid what I was eating because I knew I would get in trouble. In the moment of stuffing the food in my mouth, it felt good; it felt good for about 5 minutes afterwards and then the guilt would set in. So the endless cycle of what I now know to be Binge Eating Disorder started.

One day not very long after my Dad left, or so it seemed, I came home from school and there was a man sitting in our living room. He was introduced to me as the man who would be my Step-Dad. That is how I remember it happening. I hope it wasn't as brutal as that, I hope careful consideration had gone into how and when to introduce him to us and not to rush it, but that is not my recollection. I guess I knew it was coming after the conversation I overheard but it was still a shock. I also knew deep down that there was nothing I could do about it. It was a done deal.

My Mum and Step-Dad married when I was 7, and in what seemed a pretty short time, she changed my name by deed poll to my Step-Dad's surname and then we moved house. Away from the loving older couple who lived across the road who cared for us and were always pleased to see us. They were the perfect antidote to the venomous environment we often found at home. They didn't have children of their own and were so lovely to me and my brother.

I was asked if I wanted to change my surname and it seemed like a game to me. The exciting thing was my new surname would be the same as my best friend. We would be like sisters. So it was done, but then we moved away. To start afresh, I suppose, after the wedding but it tore me from what had been some comfort and solace in an otherwise loveless and ever changing world.

I was a bridesmaid at the wedding along with my Mum's friend. I'd had a few dress fittings where there were lots of mutterings about me needing a bigger size. My Mum said that wouldn't be necessary as she intended to put me on a crash diet. There are a few photos from that summer, 1976 I think, and I am on a beach in Wales in a bikini (the only year I had a bikini). My Mum would look at those photos over the years and comment that that was the one year I looked all right. Of course the message I took from those comments was that every other year I didn't look all right. That was the start of my belief that my body was unacceptable too.

The diet worked, and I got in the dress for the wedding in September. I was nervous, but I did good. When I got back to school the next week I wrote a story about the wedding and I said that I looked beautiful when the sun shone on me. Someone must have said that to me as it's not something I would have come up with myself. When parents' evening came around at school, my Mum and Step-Dad came home and told my brother that the teacher had shown them the story and they all had a good laugh about me saying I looked beautiful. My Mum was also cross that I wrote a story about me when it was her wedding day. Over the years, this story has been repeated quite a few times and the guffaws cut deep each time. I was ridiculed for daring to write that I looked beautiful. It seemed that even to think such a thought was outrageous in their eyes. That was the last time I ever wrote anything good about myself or believed it. I certainly never thought I was beautiful. I now have that photo of me as a bridesmaid in a frame next to my desk where I work and I smile at her every day. She smiles back. She was beautiful.

The worst thing about it all for me was that my Mum remarrying was the obvious end of any hope that my Dad might come back.

After the wedding, the house move came next, followed by 2 younger brothers over the next 3 years. We had a nice house, nice cars, a caravan and a speedboat in Wales. We had dogs, cats, rabbits, terrapins, a horse, a pony and a goat (yes a goat!). The goat was called Millie and in the winter she used to come into the kitchen and lean against the radiator to keep warm. We (as in the kids) had to keep an eye on her and when her tail went up we had to quickly get her outside! The pony used to come in too and the horse often had his head over the bottom half of the kitchen stable door looking for a bowl of tea. It was a bit of a mad house. We had all the trappings and to the outside we probably looked like one big happy family.

I wasn't happy at all. Along with the surname change and the house move, I was taken to sit the entrance exam for the private school I mentioned earlier. I wasn't asked if I wanted to go to the school, I didn't even realise what was going on when I was taken to this grand house on a Saturday morning to "do a little test". I must have passed and instead of moving onto the local middle school with my friends I had to catch a coach at 7am for this new school and I returned around 5pm. I hated it from the word go but I just did as I was told.

I joined the school in the last year of the lower school so everyone knew each other already. I went from being one of the clever ones in my old school, which gave my confidence a boost, to being average in this new school. Being one of the most capable at school was the only thing that stopped me feeling entirely worthless so to have that taken away wrecked what bit of confidence I had. I was desperate to fit in.

I started shop-lifting. I can't remember how it began, it might have been a dare or I might have been showing off saying I could do it, but soon I started taking orders from the girls at school. I usually went with a friend (she lived near me and also went to that school and our parents were friends) but sometimes I went on my own. We caught the bus into town on a Saturday and delivered the stuff at school on Monday. It was stupid stuff like stationery, sweets, hair bobbles. It made me feel good, as though I fitted in, but I knew I didn't really. They tolerated me I suppose, the nerdy new girl trying to impress.

Tolerance was unfortunately lacking in the vile girl on the school coach that made my life hell every day I went to that school. She'd push me off the seat. She'd tip my bag out all over the floor. She'd say whatever awful thing came into her head which was usually relentless teasing about me being fat and wearing glasses. That was a tough time for me. I think I told my Mum about some of it but she didn't want to know. I think I was supposed to be grateful I was going to a private school.

The shop-lifting was most weekends for quite a few weeks until one Saturday when I was out on my own and I felt a strong hand on my shoulder as I was walking out of Woolworths with lots of stolen stuff in my bag. I'd been nicked by the store detective. That was my first experience of that feeling when you know you've done something wrong and it's like your blood and breath fall to the pit of your stomach and you go cold all over before the shame floods your body and you become boiling hot.

I was marched across the store to the office at the back where I had to wait for the police to come and get me. I was shaking, scared to death about what was going to happen and most of all dreading what my Mum would say. A policeman arrived and I remember him saying he wouldn't put handcuffs on me if I promised not to run away. I couldn't run fast in normal shoes but I was wearing my fancy cowboy boots that were a size too small and killed my feet so I couldn't run if I wanted to. I was taken out the back door of the shop and put in the back of a big, black police van where I sat on the side bench with my head in my hands desperately worried about what was going to happen next.

At the police station I was taken into a room. At this point they found out I was only 10. I seem to remember the policeman was quite kind to me as he could see I was terrified. I was crying and saying that I was only stealing stuff for others and I would pay but could they please not tell my Mum. Eventually I could hear her marching down the corridor asking loudly where I was, baby on her hip. She was livid. Her face was screwed up in anger, she was bright red and if it were possible there would have been steam coming out of her ears. I think as I was 10 there wasn't much the police could do with me so they cautioned me and as soon as we could leave, my Mum stormed off leaving me hobbling along in her wake trying my best to keep up in my stupid boots.

In the car, she let rip. She screamed at me through gritted teeth, spittle landing on my face. She told me what a disgrace I was, how she couldn't even look at me and I just hung my head in shame. When we got home, without looking at me she hissed at me to go to my room. She followed me, made me pull my knickers down and lean on the bed and then she whacked me with a slipper, a big slipper with a hard rubber sole, on my bare bottom about 6 times. She was angry, really angry, and that made her even stronger than usual. I was so stunned I hardly made a sound and when she left I just sank to the floor, silent tears running down my face. I knew I'd done wrong but the hatred I felt she had for me in that moment was worse than anything I had experienced before.

Classic situation; kid's mother remarries and kid plays up. When my Mum eventually asked me why I did it, all I could say was that it was the girls at school. I think I made out that they made me do it. To be honest, how and why it started is pretty fuzzy unlike the thrashing I got which is very clear. I think on the surface, I did it to fit in at the new school but if the new school was the only thing I had to contend with at the time, would I still have done it? I'm not so sure.

The one good thing that came from the shop-lifting was that I was expelled from that school and I got to go to the local middle school after all (the one where my Mum had to grovel to the head). I was so much happier there.

None of this was my Step-Dad's fault. I didn't feel like he treated me and my brother differently but I already felt different so even if he had I'm not sure I would have noticed. On the face of it my Mum was very much in charge and he worked hard to make the money to pay for the lifestyle they enjoyed.

CHAPTER 10

It was quite magical, shimmering white, perfect in a way only an artificial Christmas tree can be. I can see brightly coloured baubles on it, magenta, purple, jade and deep pink, shining like jewels with a trim of silver tinsel. In my mind I can see the tree quite clearly, I just can't see where the tree is. It was the 70s and it could be anyone's tree. As I am trying to recall those very early Christmases, there isn't much I can remember but I am helped by some photographs my Mum gave to me.

One year me and my brother got a cardboard play shop from Father Christmas. I loved that play shop. It was like a big cardboard box, with a door kids could get through and then inside there was a counter where you could put a till and the back had a display of shelves painted on it. I have a photo of me standing behind the counter, hair in bunches, I think I'm about 4 or 5, and a big smile on my face. It's one of the few photos where I look happy.

There's another photo of me and my brother dressed as an angel (me) and a devil (him) and I'm not sure if it was for school or a party. A party I think as I'm not sure even in the 70s there would have been a school play featuring the devil! He is wearing red tights, a red long-sleeved jumper, horns on his head and he's holding a trident-like spear. I have on a sheet that our lovely neighbour had sewn together to make a big dress and edged it with silver tinsel. I don't look very happy as I heard my Mum say it would have to be a sheet sewn together as she couldn't find an angel costume that would fit. I'm a little bit older in this photo but I'm still under 7. I remember then a pervasive feeling of being trouble, problematic, something to be dealt with. I felt such guilt at my size and how hard it must be for my Mum to sort out costumes and stuff but how could I be responsible for that?

I am racking my brains trying to remember early Christmases with my Dad but the memories won't come. I feel sad that I can't remember and wonder why not. Has my survival mechanism kicked in so hard over the years to stop my feelings that it has blocked out all the memories? I hope in time to unlock more because whilst the bad memories are blocked, so are the good ones. Unfortunately blocking the memories doesn't block the feelings and some of those are very much alive and kicking.

I have more memories of the next house we lived in with my Step-Dad. At Christmas there would be lights outside on the bushes by the front door, there would be lights around the garage and the house would be elaborately decorated with a gorgeous tree, garlands, wreath on the door and lights all over the place. It looked very jolly.

We might have had one Christmas there before my youngest brothers came along, but my memories of Christmas there all involve the little ones. I don't know when it started, but me and my oldest brother opened our presents on Christmas Eve. Looking back, it might have been to give my Mum and my Step-Dad time to see us open our presents as Christmas Day was all about the little ones. I just remember always thinking they mattered more than me and my brother. It makes me sad to think of that now and it's quite possibly an unfair assumption I made but it was how I felt.

The build up to Christmas was always a mix of my Mum getting quite excited and also uptight. She had this set of Christmas lights that she put up in the kitchen and they played Christmas music. They were proper cheesy. She loved them and I secretly liked them too. My brothers weren't so keen and would turn them off at every opportunity. I would turn them back on again whenever I remembered. When I left home, sometimes my Mum would ring me up and play the music from those lights down the phone to me. I used to like that. A moment of bonding in what was otherwise a disjointed relationship. As an adult I have looked a few times to buy some lights that play music but never managed to find any.

Mostly Christmas was a stressful time in our house. We were forced to spend the day together as a family, which brought the relationships into sharp focus. It was all about my little brothers and whether my Mum would kick off and it was not a time I looked forward to. In fact, I'd go as far as saying that I hated Christmas for a long time. As I got older I could go out after we'd eaten to see friends and that eased the intensity but the memories of those Christmases loom large to this day.

As a child, all I knew was the happy family time at Christmas that I saw on the TV looked nothing like what went on in our house. We were all together on Christmas Day, supposedly having a fabulous time whereas I was hoping it would pass as quickly as possible so we could get it over with. Later on in my life my Mum told me she hated Christmas when we were all little because every year was hard trying to decide what to buy us, getting what she thought we wanted only to find we'd changed our minds. As an adult, and with children of my own, I can see now that she felt a lot of pressure at Christmas and perhaps she was trying hard to make it good for us. I don't know what her Christmases were like as a child so she may well have been trying to give us the sort of Christmas she never had. If that was the case, unfortunately all the effort just meant she hated it and it showed. She always preferred New Year when the pressure of Christmas was over.

I came to dread Christmas Day. Depending on what presents my little brothers would get, I would spend Christmas Day and Boxing Day playing with them or making whatever Lego set they'd got. I spent one Christmas making the Lego train set and that took hours. Another year it was a Lego space station. Maybe I took it upon myself to build them rather than it being expected of me? I think it was an extension of my every day need to feel useful and it became heightened with the extra emotion at Christmas.

My Mum would always cook a huge amount of food and she seemed to hate every minute of it. I'd end up helping as she got fed up or too drunk to care. We'd sit down to eat about 5pm and we'd pile our plates high. We always used to have a huge turkey from the butcher. One year the legs had to be cut off to get in the oven. Another year the oven wouldn't close properly so it was wedged shut with a brush handle rammed under it. For a change, one time, we had pheasant (pheasant was popular in the 80s) and I have a photo of my Step-Dad cutting the pheasants in half with secateurs. I think he cleaned them first! He looks happy as he smiles at the camera. I was always taking photos and it's great to have them to look back on.

The other thing about Christmas was the drinking. I would be on high alert for when the rows would start, depending on how much my Mum and Step-Dad had drunk. If we could get through the day with them both falling asleep in the chair, while I played with the little ones, that was a success. She'd start pretty early in the day and then it was only a matter of time before the descent into the mean belligerence that usually happened. Sometimes she managed to stay a happy drunk but you never could tell. It was that unknown that was hard to cope with. The hope she wouldn't turn nasty, the waiting and the highly likely disappointment when she did. Then it was every person for themselves to keep out of her way until she passed out. It was often a relief when she did pass out because we knew we had an hour or two of relative calm until she woke up. I'd usually try and tidy up and make things as nice as possible so when she woke up she might be in a good mood. It rarely worked but it gave me something to focus on I suppose.

I'd try my best to keep my Mum calm and the boys from annoying her so hopefully there wouldn't be a row. I can now see that that must have been so infuriating to my Mum, to know that I was trying to manage her like that. I am sure she wished I wouldn't do it and I wished I didn't feel the need to do it. My Step-Dad drank too but I never saw my Step-Dad's drinking as a problem; just my Mum's. Perhaps he drank in order to zone out. He didn't get mad with us like she did but they had some mad stinking rows together. Drink-fuelled rages that sent us kids scuttling to our separate rooms to hide.

It's only in the last 12 months or so that I have realised that her drinking had a massive impact on him as well. It can't have been easy. He didn't step in and protect us but I guess he didn't know what to do. He told me recently that he once said to her that maybe she was an alcoholic and needed help. Apparently she replied that she wasn't an alcoholic but she was a dipsomaniac. I had to look that word up:

Dipsomaniac – a person with an irresistible craving for alcohol
Alcoholic – a person who is unable to give up

the habit of drinking alcohol

There is a subtle difference there but it's easy to see how she was distancing herself from any responsibility and blaming it on an irresistible urge. She probably thought she was beyond help. If she had been able to dig into her emotions, I suspect there would have been a lot of shame attached to the drinking and that is what stops a lot of people with a drinking problem seeking help. Society accepts alcohol unquestionably but is quick to shame the people that fall prey to its seduction.

Whatever word she preferred, alcoholic or dipsomaniac, the impact is the same – a devastating fracturing of our family with effects that reach well into the next generation and beyond. My Gran, my Mum's mum, was an alcoholic so it is not a total surprise my Mum was. I am determined that, as far as I am able, alcoholism will not impact my children as it affected me and my brothers. Yes, I have behaviour patterns from my childhood survival strategies that I bring to my present but I am working on them every day. It is work I have to do. I am lucky as I don't seem to have inherited the need for alcohol so my fight to break the generational curse is at least not having to deal with that. Alcoholism is a symptom of something much deeper, it is a sign that healing is needed, and it is that need for healing that gets passed down generations.

The best thing about Christmas dinner for me has always been the turkey sandwiches later the same day or the day after. Probably because the stress of getting the massive meal ready is done and it's easy to just make a butty. I could also sneak more than I should when no-one was watching; to fill the gaping void inside me. That dark bit, deep inside me that was always empty.

My Mum made proper bread sauce from scratch. My Step-Dad loved it and I've always thought of it as a real part of the Christmas meal. It's so much better than the stuff you can buy in the shops. About 5 years ago I decided to make real bread sauce like my Mum had done. It tastes amazing and is well worth the effort. It also brings my Mum into Christmas in a tiny way. It is a bond with her that I relish; it is uncomplicated, easy and delicious which is everything my relationship with her wasn't.

My Mum didn't teach me to cook but I learned to cook from her. I watched, paid attention mainly so I could finish the meal off if it went pear-shaped. She was a "throw whatever you've got in the fridge or cupboard" sort of family cook and I've learned that from her. She taught me how to make white sauce using a roux and she always made lasagne with white sauce rather than cheese sauce and I do the same. It's nice to have a few little traditions that I can carry on. It helps me feel connected to my past.

My brothers and I never specifically talked about Mum's drinking or how we coped with it. We blamed each other for things if we were in trouble as we were ali so scared of her. We may have made flippant remarks to each other about keeping out of the way or "here we go again" sort of stuff but I don't remember. I just recall it being like "keep your head down, let it pass". It didn't bring us together; it sent us to our own state of survival and as adults we are working on our relationships as siblings from such a fractured beginning. The age gap didn't help as my oldest brother and I left pretty much as soon as we could at 18 and never went back. Leaving the younger ones behind. They had a tough time in other ways and in ways I don't even know about as we don't talk about it. There are times that I feel guilty about escaping when I did, but I know in my heart I had to. It was survival.

This was my experience of Christmas from 8 to 18 and it has shaped my feelings around Christmases ever since. I felt sorry for myself because I hoped for so much better and it never came. I read books with scenes of warm family Christmases, I saw similar pictures on TV and I imagined I saw the same thing when I got a glimpse of my friends' families at this time. I had a friend that I would sometimes go and see on Christmas Day. She was the oldest of 4 (like me) and all 3 of her siblings were a lot younger so I compared my situation to hers. Yet her house always seemed warm and jovial when I arrived in the evening, lots of family around, having a drink but laughing and joking and looking as if they were enjoying spending time together. When I arrived they'd greet me with hugs and smiles and ask what I'd been up to. They were interested and made me feel very welcome. It was a stark contrast to the atmosphere I'd left at home.

I went home at Christmas well into my 20s, sometimes with my then boyfriend in tow, but I didn't stay very long. It was the Christmas of 2000 when I was 31 that I finally saw the light. A lot happened in 1999 and 2000 and I wasn't in a good place so when I ended up in a row with my Mum on Christmas Eve, I left her house and went back to my flat quite prepared to spend Christmas Day on my own. As it happened, I was invited to spend Christmas with a man I'd met a couple of weeks earlier. I was going to spend the new year with him and he invited me to spend Christmas at his brother's house with their family. That was a fabulous Christmas and I remember being so carefree, I was jumping on the bed with the kids of the house dancing and singing to *Reach* (by S Club Seven) while spilling red wine everywhere (I know how to make an impression!). Yes, the company was fantastic but more than that I had said "no more" to the pain of not being enough for my mother. Being her punch bag, her focus for all her neuroses. It felt so good to do that.

6 weeks later I left the north west again and moved to Bristol to be with that man. I thought I had found something very special but it didn't last. Before it ended though we had another Christmas together in Bristol and it was yet another without the influence of my Mum. This was the time I decided to get myself off the rollercoaster that was my relationship with my Mum and distance myself.

I was emboldened by my move to Bristol and taking charge of my life more than I had ever done before. Over the years I had tried so hard to do the right thing by my Mum but I never got it right. Whatever right means. I gave up because I finally realised it was probably never going to be any better. I wish I could say that I gave up because I felt I deserved better but it would be a while yet before I got to that stage. Was I giving up? I was giving up the dream of it ever being a lovely family together. That ship had sailed. It was an act of rebellion in a way, refusal to just go along with the whole mess of our family life. It was the first time I got the real feeling that I had to break away for my own good. That not only would it probably never get better, it was getting worse; it's impact on me seemed greater once I'd had distance from it and I didn't want to go back. I had to get away.

That was the start of my withdrawal. It was a giving up of sorts but giving up of hope that things there would change. That was what I was moving away from but at the same time I felt empowered; that I was moving to something better for me. Being on my own, that Christmas I walked away, was a conscious choice and better than being in the chaos with my Mum. It felt like I stepped up and decided that I'd had enough.

No matter how much progress I think I've made since then, even though I am an adult in my 50s, Christmas still bites me in the arse. I find it really hard to relax. I am desperately trying to make Christmas for my family a very different affair but in trying so hard I make them part of an expectation that it will be fabulous. Actually just not awful will be ok. Most years I still mess it up and get upset. I suppose the plus side is I see it now, eventually. I see that in my own family I am repeating how Christmas was for my Mum. I have taken that on from her. Over the last 4 years my experience of Christmas has improved and dare I say it I even enjoy it at times. We don't always have turkey at Christmas because we don't all like it. I do make bread sauce. I don't miss the big roast dinner but I do miss the turkey butties!

CHAPTER 11

I had bought a huge rucksack for the trip. It was black, bright pink and lime green. I had packed all my stuff and repacked it about 20 times to work out how best to squeeze in as much as possible. I was going to be away for 3 months but it would be summer so I didn't need much in the way of warm clothes. I got it all in and after a bit of a struggle I could just about lift it onto my back.

After my degree, I went to law school in York for a year until July 1991 and I was due to start my training contract at a law firm in London the following May. I stayed with my then boyfriend and worked in a shop to earn some money before going back to my parents for Christmas. I had a few weeks to sort out my stuff before leaving for Australia in January. My Mum had been a pain the whole of the time I was home saying how worried she was going to be and would I be ok? I kept telling her I would be fine but it didn't help the rising nerves. I was a bit confused by this sudden display of concern from her after years of disinterest and I was annoyed that she seemed to be making it all about her. Like I was being selfish or something for making her worried. I didn't understand it and there wasn't an opportunity to talk about it as we didn't do that sort of thing, talk. So on a cold winter day I left my Mum in tears in the departure area of Manchester Airport and headed through the gates to …. well I had no idea what lay ahead. It was going to be an adventure.

Taking time off to travel was becoming popular and I heard lots of great stories about Australia so I decided I'd go there. I was going on my own and I'm not quite sure why. I don't remember talking to anyone about it or asking any of my friends if they wanted to do it. Most of my university friends had jobs to start. I also thought it would be hard being with someone 24/7 so I decided to go alone. In my heart now, as I am writing this, I think I also felt a bit like no-one would want to come with me and spend all that time with just me, so I protected myself from the rejection by not asking. There is also a part of me that thinks I would have felt unable to rely on anyone else. I was very self-sufficient. Australia was a good option as it was English speaking and

I'd heard it was safe and easy to get around. I didn't give it a huge amount of thought, it just felt the right thing to do so I bought my ticket with my 21st birthday money that I had saved for something big.

I had planned part of the trip. I was flying into Perth via Singapore (in transit only at Singapore, with no stopover). Two weeks after arrival I had a flight from Perth to Adelaide then nothing planned until my final week where I had a flight from Cairns to Sydney and then Sydney to the UK two days later. I had no accommodation booked, nothing. I had been told it was so easy to get accommodation that I just trusted that would be the case. I had never flown long haul before, let alone to the other side of the world and I was shattered by the time I arrived at Perth airport. Emotional too. The realisation that I was arriving in Perth at 2am with no plan hit me about an hour before we landed and I started to panic. I had been chatting to the nice old lady sitting next to me who was going to stay with her daughter and I hoped she might offer me a bed for the night. No such luck and as I collected my rucksack from the baggage carousel I knew I had to do something.

I wandered into the arrivals hall which was pretty empty by the time I'd faffed about going to the toilet, fixing my bag and other things I could do to waste some time. I didn't fancy the airport all night and couldn't see anyone else bedding down for a sleep so I looked around and found a board listing the backpacker's hostels. There were instructions about what to do if you arrived in the night so I called a number from a pay phone (mobile phones were still not a thing yet), being so thankful I had some loose change, and I was told by a sleepy person at the other end to get a bus that would be outside the main terminal door and it would drop me at the hostel door. Sheer desperation and a big dose of naivety helped me follow those instructions and about 45 minutes later I was being shown to an empty bed in a room where 4 other people were gently snoring and snuffling away. I just took off my clothes, got into bed and fell straight asleep.

The next day I finally woke up about 1pm to find the room empty and the place eerily quiet. I had a bit of a nosey around, found the bathroom and had a shower and then ventured downstairs. It was a big old house with doors everywhere. I was sorely tempted to open each door but I didn't want to get in trouble so I just wandered around to get my bearings. It was an old colonial style house; rectangular, 2 storeys, symmetrical with the front door in the middle and an even number of windows either side, wooden facade painted white and a chimney. Inside there were stripped wooden floors, doors and a rather grand staircase. Downstairs there was a massive kitchen with about 12 chairs around a huge wooden table. It was a bit messy but I'd seen much worse! Outside I came across a couple sitting in the shade who told me it was January 26th, Australia Day, and as it was a bank holiday everyone was out at a festival in the city. That explained why it was so quiet. They told me how to get to a local shop to get some food so off I went.

After the relative cool of the house and the garden, the wall of heat that hit me when I went out the front door took my breath away. It was intense and in my jet-lagged confusion I found it hard to grasp. I had left home in winter and arrived in this heat. I knew it was going to be hot but this was unlike anything I'd ever experienced before. I had a real moment of questioning what I had got myself into. Could I do this? Was it going to be ok?

Maybe my Mum was right and I shouldn't have come? I knew that no-one was going to swoop in and save me and I had to get on with it. I was not going to let my Mum be right.

I laid low for the rest of that day and the next one, getting over my jet lag and deciding what to do. There was always someone around so I could chat if I wanted to and it was quite pleasant. However, I hadn't come to the other side of the world to hide in a backpacker's hostel so I made myself go out on the third day. I discovered the Swan River and Fremantle and other fabulous places Perth has to offer and I began to enjoy myself. Life as a backpacker is easy if you have money for trips and things. I'd decided to work in the UK before coming out so I had money to do things while I was in Australia. I had also left my car with my Step-Dad to sell for me and he was going to pay my credit card bills as they came in. I had enough money if I was careful so after a week I booked on a trip that would take me around some of the south of Western Australia. It was very easy-going, picking people up from one location and taking them to the next with perhaps a stop on the way. I loved that part of Western Australia and it was great to be out of the city.

One night I was in a hostel close to the beach and when I say hostel it was really a lovely old wooden house. Single-storey, wide and sprawling, white with a red roof and the garden out the front was surrounded by a low wooden fence with a gate opening to the path that led up to the front door. The house had a gorgeous verandah the vast width of the front of the house; all it needed was a rocking seat to make it picture perfect in my eyes. At the back of the house was a path leading through bushes and trees to the beach. It was like something I could imagine but didn't know actually existed. I was blown away and it turned out to be the nicest hostel I stayed in.

On my first night there, a couple of girls asked me if I wanted to go for a walk with them. It was warm and still with barely any light pollution so the stars were unlike anything I had ever seen before. They twinkled against the deep midnight sky as though they were winking conspiratorially at me, somehow telling me that it was true, I was there and to believe it. We sat on the beach, which was quite narrow and banked gently down to the shore, just taking in the silence. Then we heard a noise close by, like air being pushed out of a tube. After a few moments of quiet whispering we worked out the noise was coming from the sea right in front of us. When whatever it was moved, slowly we could see its shape, and it was a dolphin really close to the shore. I was in awe of the magic of that moment. It wasn't anything I could ever have imagined happening and it took me a few moments to understand that it was real.

That was the real charm of the whole trip to Australia for me, those enchanting moments in nature witnessing something almost beyond comprehension to a small town girl like me. It somehow gave me the understanding that there was so much more out there in the world than I had experienced so far in my life and I wanted more of it. So much more. I wanted life to be different and enjoyable and full of as many joy-filled moments as I could get. I wanted something different than I had experienced so far.

Home had been hard and university and law school had been about getting the education out of the way but the next phase of work and moving to London held much more hope. The money would allow me to be independent and live life on my terms, well that was my hope. In that moment on the beach I came to appreciate that life was there for the taking, to be experienced, witnessed, absorbed, felt. It was up to me to make it happen. I was reminded of that magical feeling again a couple of nights later when I was sitting at the top of a hill outside Albany looking at the stars and I was treated to a display of shooting stars that was so incredible I thought it was fireworks at first.

My trip around the south of Western Australia came to an end and I went back to Perth for my flight to Adelaide. In Adelaide I stayed in a small hostel with just 10 beds in 1 big room and I was the only girl there. Strange thinking back, and I think I would be frightened in that situation now, but back then it was totally okay and I even had a very drunken evening with them all to celebrate my 23rd birthday. It was fun and I was, with 3 brothers and sharing a flat for 2 years at university with 3 guys, very used to being one of the boys. I think it was that hostel that I woke up one morning to see the biggest cockroach I never want to see again crawling along the wall next to my bed. That was my last night there!

I wanted to get out and about. This was my trip, my time to see the sights, explore as much as I could. I was meeting lots of people from all over the world and it was fun. I didn't eat out much and tried to eat as cheaply as I could to make the money go further for trips. I didn't drink much either, my birthday night was one of the few nights I drank, as I didn't feel safe being responsible for myself if I was drunk. As I was on my own, I thought no-one would miss me for weeks if anything happened to me.

My relationship with alcohol was quite confused at this time of my life. I did drink but in a controlled way and I often ended up being the responsible one getting people home at the end of the night. The only time I let my hair down was when I felt safe with a friend who would get me home if I needed help. Like this one time at university, I got very drunk with one of my flat mates and his friends, and after several attempts from me to make the pavement my bed, he managed to get me home. He even sat by my bed making sure I didn't choke. It says a lot about our friendship that I trusted him to look after me that night. We are still friends today.

My next trip was to Ayers Rock. Today the rock is known as Uluru which is the original name for the rock given to it by indigenous Australians. I am going to use Ayers Rock in this book only because that is what it was called at the time I am writing about. Travelling by night saved paying for a night's accommodation so I found myself wide awake on a coach in the middle of the night watching as the driver avoided the kangaroos that jumped out into his headlights. The roads were very straight and very dark so the roos looked like actors on a stage in the spotlight as we hurtled towards them. All the coaches have big bars on the front, called "roo bars", so the front of the coach doesn't get damaged if they hit one. Thankfully I didn't see any die on that night trip. It is a 17-hour drive from Adelaide to Ayers Rock and there was an overnight stopover on the way at Coober

Pedy, an opal mining town. Strange place and so very hot. Homes are dug into the ground for the cooling effect as there is no shade above ground. I found it a harsh wilderness but intriguing.

There were so many backpackers in Australia at that time, largely doing the same sort of thing, so whenever I reached a popular spot there would be lots of coaches all stopping at the same time. To look around Coober Pedy, I ended up with a group of 3 other lone travellers and we wandered around together. One of the guys was easy to get on with and we had quite a laugh. We shared the same sarcastic sense of humour. It's wonderful how we can connect with a stranger in the middle of nowhere. After a night's sleep we all headed back to our coaches and continued on to Ayers Rock.

I thought it was hot at Coober Pedy, but Ayers Rock was even hotter. The first afternoon we got there we went to look at the Olgas (another rock formation close by) and the temperature gauge in the coach showed 47 degrees. I had never experienced anything like it. It is a dry heat and stepping off the air-conditioned coach felt like stepping into a massive red hot furnace. All around was just so much heat, it almost felt like you could touch it. There was no shade. I recall thinking how amazing it was to be somewhere like that and I doubted I would ever be anywhere hotter. I was right about that.

In 2017, climbing Uluru was banned because of the spiritual significance of the site. The climb permanently closed on 26th October 2019. I totally agree with that decision but back in 1992 climbing the rock was one of the things to do so I did it.

Climbs started very early because of the heat and my group started the climb at 5 am. It was a hard climb and the first part was so steep it had a chain to hang on to. People flocked out of coaches and up the designated route like a highly organised colony of ants but, instead of gathering food, the aim was to reach the top and sign the book. I walked it with a couple of Danish girls I'd met and the picture of me signing the book at the top has the sense of accomplishment written all over my face. The view from the top was astounding. Red desert everywhere, as far as you can see in every direction. The vastness and wilderness was what struck me most about Australia. The cities are just that, cities, whereas nature is a wonder and Australia is such a huge landmass, much of it quite inhospitable, that it has been allowed to remain a wonder. Other than us ants climbing the rock for all those years of course and I am glad that it has returned to its sacred tranquillity.

The walk up was hard and the walk down was quicker but tough on the knees. As I was on my way up, the guy I had chatted to in Coober Pedy was on his way down and I made some quip about being careful of his old knees (he was only 2 years older than me but that's enough for a joke, right?). He will no doubt have said something sarcastic in return and he was off back to his coach.

When I got off the coach at that night's hostel I bumped into him again and we agreed to meet up later on. It was nice to see a friendly face and feel like I sort of knew someone. After a rest I met him as planned and we spent the evening having a good old laugh. He was tall and dark-haired and made me laugh and yes I found him attractive but nothing happened for 2 reasons – I am awful at reading signals and had no idea what he thought about me and I would never have the confidence to make a move but, more importantly, I was technically still with my law school boyfriend, although I hadn't had a letter from him yet and I was sensing things weren't going well. It was just as friends we enjoyed each other's company. I also remember we walked into Alice Springs together and I think that might have been the next day. He was due home in the UK before me but he lived in Kent and as I was moving to London we agreed to meet up sometime later in the year. We swapped addresses, actual postal addresses as email wasn't a thing then. He left the next morning and I went to wave him off. I left later that day on an overnight coach back to Adelaide.

In Adelaide I promptly booked my next trip and left the next day on a five-night trip to Melbourne. It was a minibus of 11 girls and a driver all doing the same trip and it was nice to be with the same people for a few days. Meeting new people all the time is really interesting but it is also exhausting so it was good to have a rest from that. We made various stops along the way and the scenery was stunning. The end part of the trip was the famous Great Ocean Road which is jaw-droppingly gorgeous. The sea there is so blue. I haven't seen views like that since.

On that trip I met a girl I got on well with so we spent another week together in and around Melbourne and horse-riding in the hills above the city. The scenery was stunning and it was the only time I saw a massive snake, a highly venomous brown snake. My horse saw it first as it nearly threw me off when it saw the snake and reared. I managed to stay on and the snake slithered away, unperturbed.

I think it was in Melbourne that all the letters from my boyfriend and my Mum arrived at the post office and I felt homesick reading all the news from my Mum. I was homesick for something familiar rather than home itself. I longed for somewhere to belong. The letters from my boyfriend were in answer to all the ranty letters I'd written to him about why hadn't he written to me. I cringe now at how insecure I was and unpleasant at times, fuelled by that insecurity. It showed itself in my fierce defence of myself, in my "fuck you if you don't want me anymore" assumption at his lack of correspondence. I was hurting but making myself most unlikeable in the process. He was busy with work and getting on with his life while I gadded around Australia. Writing letters to me to keep me feeling happy wasn't top of his to-do list every day and I don't blame him now, looking back on it. At the time I thought he'd found someone else - I mean why would he wait for me? – so I acted out. My dark thoughts surrounding that relationship were a blot on my Australia trip and they were all of my own making but I didn't see it like that at the time.

After Melbourne I took a coach to Canberra where I arrived at 5am to a deathly quiet city that felt like it had been dropped into the landscape, ready-made. I was very tired after a night on a coach and only had a few hours in Canberra before my coach left for Sydney. I walked up to Capital Hill (now known as Parliament House I believe) and back and the streets all looked as though the buildings had been built at the same time. Same style and not very interesting to me. I'm sure there is much more to Canberra than what I saw and I also think I was getting city fatigue by then. It was the natural sights that I wanted to see. In Sydney I hung out with some girls I met and we saw the city sights, went to the Hard Rock Café, Manly and the Aquarium, the Blue Mountains and Bondi Beach. They were best friends and didn't mind having me tag along.

It was just outside Sydney that I went hang gliding. I love trying as many things as I can so a tandem hang glide, where I get to enjoy the experience but not have to learn how to do it, seemed perfect. I thought the launching off the cliff into the air would be the hard bit but it was so windy we were up in the air before we got near the edge. I was in the capable hands of an experienced pilot and I loved it. He wasn't a talker so I enjoyed the peace of flying like a bird, soaring the skies, gracefully. The rush of the wind on my face and the sheer exhilaration of it was fabulous. I felt so free. Getting down was a bit tricky. The wind was strong and I had to take my feet out of the strap that kept them stretched out behind me so they could dangle down. That made the harness I was wearing press onto my stomach and then he had to steer us round and round in circles …. and round and round …. again and again. By the time we got down I felt so sick and dizzy but it was good to feel the ground. It also felt amazing to have done that.

All the time I was away I would phone home every two weeks or so and each time my Mum would tell me how she wasn't sleeping with me away but at least the house was clean as she spent the time cleaning to keep her busy. Hoovering at 4am didn't go down well with the others in the house. When I told her I had been hang gliding she gave me a lecture on how dangerous that could have been and I could have died. So I didn't tell her about anything else remotely dangerous after that. Travelling on your own is great as you only have yourself to answer to but it is sometimes nice to share the memories with someone. I wish I'd kept a journal now but I do have photographs.

From Sydney I headed north making my way to Cairns. First stop was Byron Bay which was a laid-back surfing haven then. It is much bigger now I believe. Then onto Brisbane but

I didn't stay long. Next stop was Noosa on the Sunshine Coast and I took a camping trip to Fraser Island with a group of 7 for 3 nights. That was a laugh especially when the dingoes tried stealing all our shoes one night. It was like an island paradise, white sand and blue sea. It was gorgeous. Then I went on a 2-night sailing trip around the Whitsundays, a group of islands, some of them very exclusive. Now I'm not good on boats but the sea along that coast is just mesmerising and pretty calm, luckily. I also visited Magnetic Island and Dunk Island. There is so much to do along the east coast of Australia which is why it's so popular. I'm glad I went and did those things but it was a well-trodden route back then and there were other things I did, especially south of Perth that were different but just as good.

Finally, I arrived in Cairns and I was getting to the end of my trip. First activity was something I had been waiting to do - a bungee jump. I'd heard people talking about bungee jumping and it sounded amazing. Crazy but amazing. I love amusement park rides so to be tied at the ankles and jump out into the air seemed like the ultimate adrenaline rush. I wanted to do it so as soon as I got to Cairns I got myself on a mini-bus from the hostel with some other people and headed out to see what it was all about.

I didn't tell the others I was thinking of having a go; as far as they were concerned I was just going to pass time and to watch all the crazy people jumping. I definitely didn't tell my Mum! I watched a few people jump and listened with great delight as the guy in our group gradually talked himself out of it. I had purposely not told anyone so there was no pressure on me to do it. It looked quite safe and logic told me that day in day out people jumped off the platform and survived so there was no reason I wouldn't survive too.

Without telling anyone I sneaked off to pay and sign my life away on the waiver form. I was pointed in the direction of a wooden staircase at the back of the jumping platform and told to walk up until I reached the top where I would be met by someone. So I walked up the steps. They were open steps and as I walked I could see I was level with the tops of the trees and then I was getting higher and higher. About half way up I started to get nervous and I distracted myself by singing *Zip-a-dee-doo-dah, zip-a-dee-ay, My, oh, my, what a wonderful day, Plenty of sunshine headin' my way, Zip-a-dee-doo-dah, zip-a-dee-ay*. I have no idea why that song came to mind but the distraction worked and soon I was on the platform 50m above the lagoon below.

My heart is pumping hard at this stage and my legs are getting a bit wobbly. Ok, very wobbly. I am starting to doubt I can do it but luckily I am next in line and a nice man is tying the harness around my ankles and telling me it would be a good idea to tuck my t-shirt in if I didn't want to show everyone my bra. That made me laugh and eased the tension a bit. Once you are strapped in it's hard to move and all you can do is take little hops. So I am 50 metres up, tied at the ankles and I have to hop out along a wooden plank that is just a bit wider than my feet and there is nothing on either side of the plank other than a long way down. There is a rail for the first couple of hops but then I have to lean back to hold onto the rail at the same time as hopping forwards. I am beginning to regret the bravado that got me up there but at the same time I really want to do it. I take a deep breath and let go of the rail. I am now standing at the end of the plank and I refuse to look down. The guy starts to count back from 5 but at 2 I've had enough and I jump. Actually I lean forward and sort of fall forward; it was not the elegant swan dive I had in mind but it was better than the epic failure and walk back off the plank that would have happened if I hadn't gone when I did. I free fall for just a few seconds and my mind is just beginning to think "Has this rope got me?" when the rope tightened gently around my ankles and I started to bounce up and down at the end of the big elastic band I am tied to. I've done it and I am alive. I hear a loud laugh and then realise it's coming from me. I am so relieved I did it that I am laughing out loud and then I hear the people who I came with shouting to me and clapping and they all look so surprised. I like that attention, for doing a mad thing and daring to do it. A man comes out into the middle of the lagoon in a rubber boat and holds up a pole for me to grab and he pulls me down into the boat. It's all I can do to lie on my back still laughing loudly as he unties my ankles and guides the boat back to the bank. My legs are shaking as he helps me out and I am pleased to feel my feet on solid ground again. That was a great experience.

I didn't like Cairns much but there were lots of great things to do. I only had a few days so my last trip was a day boat trip to dive on the Great Barrier Reef. I've never dived before and may never dive again so I figured if I'm going to do it once I might as well do it in the most amazing place. There were about 12 of us on the boat, all non-divers, so we went down with an experienced diver who checked all our equipment for us. We had to learn very basic hand signals and I will always remember being shown what they said was the most important – thumb and index finger straight up on both hands in front of you, other fingers down. Bring the tips of the two thumbs together and that's a W. Then keep the thumbs together, move the two index fingers round to touch each other and pull the thumbs down slightly – that's a O. Pull the index fingers back out again and thumbs up to another W. Put it all together – W O W. I still love that today. I was a bit nervous about feeling claustrophobic when we got underwater but it was absolutely fine and I totally loved it. Even though we only went down about 10 metres, the coral and the fish were just incredible. It was like a secret world under the sea and it felt such a privilege to visit it that day. I saw clown fish nestling in the coral, just like Nemo (although Finding Nemo was still many years away at that time). I came face to face with a 2 metre Grouper fish which was …. interesting. We saw reef sharks and we had been told they wouldn't harm us but, much as I loved seeing them, I was happy when they swam away. The colours were so bright and vivid and it's so sad to think how much coral reefs are struggling to survive today.

We were under the water for about 45 minutes and I had used the W O W signal pretty much non-stop but on the way back to the boat the guy I was diving with pointed to something and beckoned for me to follow him. Just a short distance away I saw a giant clam, about a metre tall, it was open and air bubbles were pouring out of it like a full on bubble machine at a kid's birthday party but a million times better. The diver very gently put his hand into the open space between the shell sides and the clam's early warning system obviously sensed something because immediately the shell started to close. It was pure magic to watch that happening, another thing that I would only ever have imagined seeing in a film or on TV, not in real-life right before my eyes. It was magnificent, so much so I forgot the W O W. Back on the boat we took all our gear off and excitedly swapped stories of what we'd seen. A few beers were consumed on the way back to land in celebration of a fantastic day.

So my trip was at an end and I packed up to fly back to Sydney. I had 2 more days there to do a bit of shopping but my credit card was refused so I phoned home to discover my Step-Dad had been driving my car and hadn't sold it. He hadn't paid my credit card bills either so I had just enough money for food and accommodation until I left. I was really cross that I could have been left stranded without access to any money but in the end it had worked out ok so no harm done. It was a stark reminder of the chaos I was flying home to and the comparison to the 3 months of utter freedom and largely joy I had just experienced was quite profound. I had a job to go back for and no money to stay but if someone had offered me an easy way to stay then I think I would have taken it.

I flew from Sydney to Heathrow via Mumbai and then on the shuttle from Heathrow to Manchester. Back in Manchester, after a long wait, I discovered that after carrying my rucksack all over Australia with me it had been lost somewhere on the way back. I laughed, it was so ridiculous. My rucksack was at Heathrow apparently even though it had been checked in through to Manchester so the airline delivered it back to me the day after.

By the time I got out through customs my Mum was annoyed because of the delay. When we got home there was a letter from my boyfriend ending it. Welcome home Philippa!

It was actually the kick I needed to get my act together, find somewhere to live in London and move down there ready to start my job as a trainee solicitor.

I got in touch with this ex-boyfriend very briefly in 2020 as I wanted to help someone I know to get a training contract in a criminal law firm. I had followed my ex's career a little bit as he was a criminal lawyer, so I was feeling brave and wrote him a note that I sent to his firm asking him to contact me if he could help. We had a brief email conversation and I put my friend in touch with him. That was that, but it was good to know he had contacted me, and even if it was just out of curiosity, he had been willing to do it so couldn't hate me that much. After all the years that have passed, it would be odd if he still hated me anyway, and he very much had the moral high ground after we split.

I was clearing out our attic in 2019 and I found a pile of letters I'd kept from him when I was travelling in Australia. It was strange seeing the end of our relationship unfurl on the pages and it was a little unsettling to see how in tune with himself he was and how I was so much in the opposite place. Unsure, unhappy, unable to trust. He ended the relationship saying it was right for him. It was the right thing for me too, but I didn't feel it at the time.

CHAPTER 12

In May 1992, at the age of 23, I moved to London and started my 2-year training contract as a trainee solicitor. Growing up, I definitely felt that if I was going to be safe, it would have to be me that made it that way. I think that's a big part of the reason I chose to do law because it would lead to a steady, secure job, although I wasn't aware I was choosing it for that reason at the time. I had done a law degree, then a year at law school and in those days that was the academics out of the way (except a compulsory law society course in year 1 and year 3 after qualification). Next came 2 years on the job training.

Until the late 80s, this part of the training had been known as "Articles", and you were known as an "Articled Clerk". The term Articles refers to the Articles of Clerkship which was the contract agreed between the Articled Clerk and the principal solicitor who agreed to train the clerk. In 1990 this was changed to a "Training Contract" to bring the language in line with more modern practice. In 1992 most lawyers still called it Articles and some still do, even today. The training involves working in different areas of law depending on what was available at your firm.

I had been interviewed at university and secured a job with the London law firm that I wanted. A big firm, not one of the really big firms but a good name all the same. I don't think I appreciated at the time how well I had done to secure that job. The firm doesn't exist anymore as it has merged many times since I left. It was a commercial law firm on the edge of the City and it acted for large commercial enterprises. When I was there, there were about 35 trainees in each year, so around 70 in total, and in most firms trainees moved departments every 6 months. Each stint in a department was called a "seat", and over 2 years, trainees would have 4 seats. The firm I went to was experimenting with four-month seats, which is why I started in May. They flipped between four-month and six-month seats while I was there.

During my first week at the firm I was given the talk all new female trainees get about not wearing trousers. I kid you not! We were told that we could only wear skirts or dresses and we would be sent home to change if we came to the office dressed inappropriately. That seems so archaic now, I know, but the dress code was still the same when I left 3 years later.

My first seat was from May to September 1992 in professional negligence litigation, mainly accountants' negligence. I was only 1 of 2 trainees starting that May and all the other trainees had at least a couple of seats under their belts by then. It was a real shock to be working in a big corporate law firm in London and I had to pinch myself sometimes to check that it was actually happening. I'd get the tube and come out at Tower Hill station just across from the Tower of London for a short 5-minute walk to the office. I'd look over to the Tower, hardly believing that I was here, in London.

Trainees always shared an office with someone, usually the person they worked for or someone in the team. I shared an office in that first seat with a nice guy who was quite young and I seem to remember we talked about music quite a lot. I had tasks like research and maintaining a database of claims to keep me busy and the 4 months sped by.

During that initial seat I came across one of the older partners, a man. He had one of the smaller offices as he was too important to share with anyone and also he smoked; smoking in offices hadn't been banned yet and his room stank. I had to go and get some papers from him one day and as he handed them over to me he commented "Not only do we let women in here now, we have northerners I see". I was so shocked I just rushed away. It was one of the few times I came across such blatant disrespect for me as a woman and as a northerner but I am sure it happened many times on the quiet.

In my first week at university (in Birmingham, the Midlands) I had been astounded when a posh southern boy expressed surprise to come across a northerner and whilst I didn't take much notice as there were, of course, lots of northerners, the exchange stuck with me.

Experiencing this again as I started my career was surprising but later in my career I found that people tended to underestimate me when they realised I was a northerner and that worked in my favour most of the time!

In September I was asked to go to the Bristol office for 6 months as my second seat.

I jumped at the chance. They put me up in a flat so I could afford to keep my flat on in London so I would have somewhere to move back to. The seat in Bristol was professional negligence litigation again, but this time dealing with claims against surveyors. It was for 6 months as it took at least 2 months to settle in and begin to be useful so they only took trainees for 6 months. This was a much more hands-on seat and I shared an office with the partner I worked for. He was a most formidable character, very tall, broad, ex-navy, a real presence and a force to contend with. I learned towards the end of my time there that they didn't usually send first year trainees to that seat as the partner in charge would only have "more useful" trainees in their second year but they agreed to have me and it went well.

I was much more involved in the cases, reviewing the surveyor's case notes, writing reports and once driving to Cornwall on my own to take a witness statement which I thought was so cool (especially as the partner sent me in his brand new Golf GTi – that car was great fun!). He gave me the lecture that he gave all trainees about the perils of paperclips - from his time in the Navy he had learned that paperclips are to be avoided at all costs as papers held together with a paperclip can easily get other papers attached to them that aren't meant to be there. There is probably much more to that story than he let on but it has stayed with me. The Bristol office was small so I got to know everyone and it was hard to leave there and go back to the big London office. I suppose I felt safe in that small Bristol office.

I went back to another 6-month seat, this time in corporate working with a woman partner that was known for being difficult, especially with other women. She was out of the office a lot and she worked weird hours sending emails in the middle of the night asking me to do certain jobs the next day. She was often unavailable during the day so if I wasn't sure what to do I had to guess. Not so much a 'hands-on' seat that one, but a 'learn to deal with a difficult boss' seat. Luckily her secretary was in every day and she was just fantastic. She had a lot of experience and often helped me work out what was needed if I was struggling. I suppose my people-pleasing tendencies came in handy here as I tried hard to keep the partner happy. I often think about that experience working for her as an example of how not to be a boss.

The next seat was in corporate banking and insolvency for 4 months. I sat with a senior solicitor who was very good at what he did even though I'm not exactly sure what that was. Working in a big corporate firm as a trainee you get involved in small parts of huge deals so you often don't get to see the big picture. I was pretty sure I didn't want to stay in banking when I qualified so I worked hard and did what I had to do, but that was all. There were lots of late nights in that seat, leaving at 4am was not uncommon being back by 9.30am. It was part of the job and I actually thought it was quite exciting back then. More like exploitative. He was much easier and nicer to work for, after the woman partner in corporate, which renewed my faith in being a lawyer.

After banking I went to commercial property for the last 4 months. Commercial property is now usually called Real Estate, following the Americans, but it was still commercial property when I was there. I shared an office with an ambitious woman on the verge of partnership and learned a lot from her. I watched her from my side of the room meticulously collate all the information she needed to prove her case for partnership (there were a lot of hoops to jump through) and have furtive conversations with her boss who was supporting her. I saw how determined and driven she was. I saw what it took to make it to partnership. I wasn't sure, even then, that I wanted it for myself. I didn't recognise anything of me in what I saw in her. She spoke with that no accent sort of posh voice, she was tall and slim, short blond hair, always meticulously dressed but in an understated almost subdued way. She seemed to glide effortlessly along the corridors, leaving a faint waft of some undoubtedly very expensive perfume behind her. I was very much in awe of her. Very occasionally she'd wear a shorter than usual skirt, or something that showed her figure off more, but those days were rare. It seemed to me she was hiding her femininity at work.

There was another woman on the same floor who was a partner and she had a reputation for being somewhat strange. She had long, dark, bedraggled hair that was all the same length and the long fringe was tucked behind her ears. She always wore dark coloured skirt suits with a straight but not tight knee length skirt and occasionally she wore an olive green, tartan 3-piece skirt suit that I thought must be for special occasions. She didn't share an office with anyone as she refused to and she rarely smiled. She was pretty scary to a young trainee like me but everyone talked about her with such reverence that I knew she was good at her job. She left an impression too and she was another woman that seemed to be in denial of her femininity. I was a bit confused about how to be a woman, be good at your job and be respected without denying your femininity. It was an added layer of confusion for me in my 20s.

Upon successful completion of those 2 years of training, I qualified as a solicitor. The training contract came to an end and the big deal then was seeing if the firm would offer me a job on qualification. I qualified in 1994 just as property was improving from the late 80s recession. I enjoyed the property seat as I liked the tangible nature of the work - I could drive round London and point to buildings and say "I bought that office block for a client last week" or "I'm in the middle of preparing the auction pack for that shopping centre" – and my boss was firm but fair, and I learned so much from her. She had just been made a partner and I was offered a job on qualification as her assistant. I was over the moon. To finally qualify as a solicitor and have a job was such a great feeling, a feeling of safety and security. I could pay my bills and look after myself. I wouldn't have to ask my family for any help.

I have never asked them for a penny since I left home to go to university. My grandfather gave me money while I was at university and he bought me a car and kept it running. That was his idea of "making sure I was looked after" as he had promised my Dad. I didn't get anything at all from my parents. I understand that sounds like I was lucky, and I do appreciate how amazing it was to leave university with no debt, but the downside was that it distanced me yet further from my parents and it felt like they took very little interest in me. Not that giving me money would have meant they were more interested but it felt like it created a divide. Whatever it was, something made me very self-sufficient; probably the chaos at home, the constant being on high alert for the situation getting out of hand and tempers fraying. I didn't feel safe at home, that's for sure, and I also knew I couldn't rely on them.

CHAPTER 13

When I moved to London to start my training contract, it was after my travels and my break up and with no real emotional support, on the back of a childhood that lacked love, warmth, security, trust and support. At work you were just expected to get on with it and it wasn't the done thing to need a lot of help. If I had needed help I wouldn't have known how to ask for it anyway. I just kept my head down and didn't let anyone know when I was finding it tough. As I started out of sync with the majority of the trainees who had started in September I felt under pressure to perform as well as they did. To find a place to live, I had answered an ad for a flat-mate and was living in Clapham in a flat with 3 girls who already knew each other. All of this fanned the flames of my "not fitting in" agony and this is where the mask that I had worn came off and out came the full suit of armour that I would stay behind for the next 25 years or so.

There were countless good times in those years, so it isn't all doom and gloom, but it took me many years to realise that I was constantly searching for a way to somehow be both acceptable and accepted but perhaps most importantly searching for something or someone or someplace to make me feel safe and secure.

I tried many jobs. From qualification in 1994 to 2001, when I started a long-term job, I had 7 jobs in either London, Manchester/Stockport or Bristol. I heard recently that the average person now stays in a job for 18 months. In the 1990s, it would have been longer, but even by today's standards, I moved around a lot.

I stayed in London for a year after qualifying as a solicitor; in the last 6 months there, I moved out of the flat I shared with the party girls and lived on my own in a studio flat. I moved out because I didn't want to go out as often and as late anymore, but the others did.

Life as a newly qualified solicitor is pretty hard work, long hours, demanding bosses and clients, and, in the 90s, not much support. The training contract period is hard, but you are usually not solely responsible for files and are mainly helping. It doesn't mean it's easier, but the buck usually stops with someone else. The minute you qualify, you get your own files and all of a sudden, the buck does stop with you. It's pretty overwhelming at times.

Others might have fared better but I didn't know how to ask for help and it certainly wasn't openly on offer. When my flat mates came in late most nights, making lots of noise and bringing goodness knows who with them, I couldn't take it anymore. It wasn't their fault. My situation had changed, not theirs. I was now earning enough money to live on my own. I was also aware that I was drinking a lot with them at weekends and probably some distance from that would be a good thing.

My new flat was clean, tidy and quiet, but I was lonely. Monday to Friday I worked long hours and could socialise after work, but weekends were harder and I missed the days of lazing around in PJs chatting and going out.

I was quite lucky as my boss was tough, but she was fair. She explained things, so I usually knew what I was doing and why I was doing it. Not everyone was that lucky. When I say she explained things, she was out of the office much of the time, so we communicated via post-it notes stuck on documents (like a lease – usually at least 80 pages long – or contract) left in a tray on her desk. I'd look a document over, form my ideas on what needed changing, put post-it notes on the relevant pages with my comments and she would look at them as soon as she could and answer my queries/comments on the post-its and leave it on my desk. I quickly got used to asking the questions or making comments in a way that elicited the information I needed to get on with the transaction. It was a strange way of working, with not a huge amount of actual face to face communication, but I learned a lot, and on the whole I liked the job.

After a year or so it was getting quite boring and being lonely living on my own didn't help so I decided to leave. When I qualified as a property lawyer in 1994, there weren't many people qualifying into property, so I was part of quite a small pool and luckily for me I always found it easy to get a job. So no sooner had I decided to leave, I was moving to Bristol to start my new job there. I can't remember why I chose Bristol; I wanted to leave London and to do the work I did it had to be a firm in a city. I didn't want to go north, I didn't fancy Birmingham, so I suppose Bristol was the obvious choice. It might well have had something to do with feeling safe there when I went as a trainee.

That job in Bristol was very different as it was smaller value transactions and the clients were less sophisticated, so I had to spend more time explaining things to them. I liked that and it made me hone my skills. I had to know what I was doing to be able to explain it clearly. The clients didn't always read reports or listen to advice, but as soon as something went wrong, they cared then, and you had to make sure you'd covered your arse. This was my second time in Bristol and I stayed exactly a year.

During my time there, my Mum and Step-Dad were having a terrible time, and I went home a lot to see if I could do anything to help. I mainly went to be there for my youngest brothers, who were 10 and 13 years younger than me and still at school. They were only 5 and 8 when I left home and I felt responsible. I have no idea why I felt that responsibility. It was something that was always in me, and I suspect it was to do with my Mum's drinking. I picked up the pieces a lot when my Mum drank too much and I felt the need to help. I also felt the need to be part of the family. I had gradually gone home less and less over the last 8 years, but I still had the yearning to be part of a loving family. The sort of family I saw other people had and badly wanted for myself.

In 1996, with hope in my heart, I left Bristol and moved back to my home town in the north west to live near my family. My Mum and Step-Dad were still just about together but it wasn't going well. My youngest brothers were 14 and 17. I had flat warming parties and I have pictures of everyone dancing on the kitchen counter, arms in the air singing loudly and having a good time. My Mum wanted to paint the flat for me, and she wanted paying in wine! I'd come home from work each day praying she wouldn't be prostrate on the floor having fallen off a ladder. I never did find her like that, but it was touch and go at times, apparently! It seems strange now to write about paying her in wine as I would have given anything for her to stop drinking but the reality is I would also do anything to stay in her good books, so wine it was.

CHAPTER 14

When I moved to London I met up with the guy I'd met in Australia (I'm going to call him Ayers Rock Guy – I think he'd like being called that) and we had fun together. I'm not sure how serious it was in his eyes but I loved the time we spent together. He wasn't sure where his career was going at that stage and he was living at home in Kent to save money. We would see each other most weeks but he was very close to his family and it made me feel insecure. I didn't know how to behave in a close family and I didn't understand the dynamic. It made me feel very nervous and sort of like I somehow had to compete. I had to be good enough to deserve his attention and I obviously found myself lacking on that front due to my low self-esteem. We had lots of fun for a few months before it ended.

The first time I met his mum and sister we all went out for a Chinese meal. I hadn't eaten much Chinese food and I had never been to a proper Chinese restaurant. I ordered Szechuan chicken much to everyone's amusement when I realised how hot it was and drank every drink on the table trying to cool my mouth down. Remember me saying how I can make an impression! I think I ended it probably because I wanted him to be around more which just wasn't possible.

There were other dalliances during my time in London but nothing serious. It was a fun time and I wasn't looking for anything serious to get in the way of my working and playing hard. What I wasn't doing, though, was being discerning and spending my time with men who treated me well. I was grateful for any sort of attention, and as a result I ended up in situations at times that I would rather not have been. I was drinking a lot and sometimes woke up in houses that I had no idea how I'd got there. It's not something I'm proud of. I'm not saying anything happened against my will but what I am saying is that I didn't respect myself enough to look out for my welfare and my safety. There were situations that left me feeling really bad about myself.

You know those questions you see sometimes along the lines of "what advice would you give your 25-year-old self?" Well, mine would be to have more respect for myself. I was easy prey, though, and I had no self-worth to stop me fawning at the attention of men, particularly men already in relationships who seemed to like flirting outrageously with me. I lapped it up. It makes me feel sick now to think about it. Their partners must have hated me, but they probably just felt sorry for me; after all, I was the one left on my own at the end of the night.

There was one guy who was a friend of the group I hung around with and he lived abroad and only came out occasionally. I'd sometimes end up with him at the end of the night, but I didn't feel rubbish when he left the next day. I've finally realised that it was because I never thought it would lead to anything more anyway. He had a life elsewhere, so we just had fun when he was in town. We'd get a cab late at night and find an all-night cafe and drink and talk. It was so exciting. He would take charge and I felt safe with him. Nothing physical ever happened with him other than a kiss and a fumble. It wasn't real, though, so in some ways, it was safe. I didn't expect anything. It makes me emotional writing this because I feel so sorry for that girl who didn't think she was worth excitement and being kept safe. At least he was nice to me. The men I fawned after and hoped for more with were always reckless (and feckless!) and not what I wanted.

CHAPTER 15

When I moved to the north west from Bristol I had managed to get a job in Manchester, about 25 miles away. I was due to start on 17th June 1996 but a terrorist bomb went off on 15th June in the Arndale Centre and the office was closed on the Monday while it was checked for structural damage. The office was fine but the car park shutter door, which was on the side of the building nearest the Arndale Centre, had a massive dent in it from the blast. I started on the Tuesday instead.

I don't remember being too bothered about the bomb. I didn't live in Manchester and I wasn't that familiar with Manchester so it didn't mean much to me as a place and there had been no fatalities, although many people were hurt. When I lived in London there were frequent bomb scares on the tube and we'd sit in tunnels for hours sometimes waiting to get moving. It was something I was used to I suppose although I had never been that close to an actual bomb site. To be honest I was so consumed with what was going on at home and my new job that I didn't have much headspace left for anything else.

My journey to the office was from the opposite side to the Arndale Centre so I didn't see the devastation. However, for my entire time at that job I could hear windows smashing and walls being pulled down as the site was cleared and the reconstruction was still underway when I left. It was gruelling, messy work going on outside the office as I was grappling with what was going on inside the office.

I was taken on in a new role as they needed another lawyer but they didn't know where to put me to start with. I'd only been qualified for 2 years and still had so much to learn, especially about people. I worked for one person, then another and then another and I began to think it was because no-one liked me or I wasn't any good. When I left, I found out that when I arrived they thought I was very good so a few of the senior people wanted me to work for them. By now, I worked on my own files so when I say I worked for them I mean that I worked on jobs for their clients. Solicitors are very protective of their client relationships, especially in big commercial firms, because having a good client base that you can call your own is what makes you valuable. It's what will hopefully help you reach the holy grail of partnership.

Traditionally there are two types of partnership: salaried partnership where you are a partner in name so you share in the responsibilities of being in a partnership but you take a salary (a very good salary mind you) and equity partnership where you take a share of the equity (profits). Some firms will have equity partners with different sized shares of the equity. Being a solicitor is paid well but the mega-bucks are in full-share equity partnership.

The firm I went to work at in Manchester had a lot of salaried partners and only a few equity partners so the salaried partners were all fighting to get a good client base and make equity. It was ruthless. When I arrived they saw me as an asset to boost their equity bid. I was pulled here and there and nearly always had too much work. I didn't want to let people down so I worked long days to get work done. I had moved to the north west to see more of my family but I wasn't able to see them during the week as I got home too late and at weekends I was shattered.

One night I was walking back to the car

park in the dark, it was late and this man walked towards me with an odd look on his face. As we got closer I sensed something was wrong and he was walking on a line that would be right next to me if he kept going. As he walked past me he grabbed my handbag and went to run away. My bag had a long strap so when he grabbed it the strap ran down my arm and into my hand. I managed to grab it and we ended up in a tug of war over my bag for what seemed like ages but in reality it was only a few seconds until someone came round the corner. He dropped my bag and ran off. Whilst he was trying to get the bag off me he was staring at me and I can see his face to this day, sullen dark eyes staring at me menacingly.

I hadn't made a sound the whole time, I hadn't shouted or anything. I was so shocked. When he went I just stood there for a minute or so before picking my bag up and walking to the car park. I was fine until the next day at work when I recounted the story, people said I should have let him have the bag; he could have stabbed me, anything could have happened. That together with the delayed shock meant I had nightmares for about 6 months and for a good 3 years afterwards every time someone came too near me in public I would jump and once I even squealed. I was so embarrassed. I didn't tell anyone what was happening and how anxious I was, I just got on with it, I didn't want to be any trouble. To be fair to them, when the big bosses heard about what happened they paid for me to have a parking space in a much closer and safer car park. I'd already changed car parks by then but it was so much nicer going to a well-lit one closer to the office.

That job in Manchester nearly broke me. After working for a lot of different people, I got told that I would be working on a deal with one of the big bosses in the team. He had a reputation for being tough and a bully. He also had a reputation for being a lady's man and was rumoured to be sleeping with one of the other junior solicitors. I was on my guard. I was going to work with him on the purchase of a business involving quite a few properties. I had to put a report together on all the properties including searches, leases and other important information. It was a big job. I worked hard but he was out of the office a lot (playing golf or other activities?!) so I couldn't run anything by him until he came back to the office. Sometimes that wasn't until late afternoon. When he did come back there was always a queue of people wanting to talk to him and I just politely waited. And waited. Sometimes I was there until 7 or 8pm. When I was finally granted an audience I'd go into his room where he sat on his big chair behind his huge desk, his shirt buttons pulling across his ample stomach (no doubt full after a nice late lunch) and I'd tell him things I had discovered and he'd yell at me. Full blown yelling about how stupid I was, why hadn't I told him sooner, if it was a problem how was it going to be fixed and any number of other things he complained about. I had never been treated like that at work before. I got enough of that treatment from my mother, but to face it at work was devastating. The chaos, the bullying, the never knowing what was going to happen next. It was reliving the trauma of my childhood but at work which until then had been my safe space.

I became very anxious, I started to make mistakes and one day I broke down in tears in front of him. I told him I was on edge all the time. His response was that I wasn't the first and I wouldn't be the last and he walked out of my office chuckling. Luckily I didn't share an office then and I closed the door and wept. I finished that job for him but didn't work on any more.

I lasted 18 months in that job and when I left I was the second longest-serving assistant solicitor in the department. Says a lot. During my time there, I found out that a guy at my level was being paid £10,000 pa more than me. I couldn't believe it. Until then, I hadn't felt a gender pay gap; I was probably very naive, but also the firms I had worked for previously had set bands for salary, so I don't think the difference would have been that great. What all firms do, though, or rather did as I can't speak for what they are like now, was encourage staff not to speak about salary. Make it a taboo subject. Us British people have a problem talking about money anyway, so on the whole, it wasn't hard to get people to keep quiet. Of course, the firm's benefitted from this silence; the staff didn't. It's always the way, isn't it? When someone wants to keep information closed rather than be transparent, there will always be winners and losers. So I raised the issue of the salary difference, and guess what? I immediately got a £10,000 pa pay rise. Not back-dated, of course, as that would imply something had been amiss. I stayed a little longer after the rise but left to move to Surrey.

Not long after I moved back to the north west, I joined an introduction agency. The forerunner to dating sites, I suppose. I can't remember much about it or the cost, but it can't have been that much. I must have filled in a form with info about me and I was matched to meet the first guy who I met for a curry. He chose a curry so hot his nose ran constantly. He spent the whole night apologising. I seem to remember he was into climbing but that's about all I can remember as well as the running nose. We didn't see each other again!

I was then matched with another guy and one cold afternoon in spring we met to go for a walk in a nearby park, at his request. The park was down the road from where I lived and about 6 miles from where he lived. I can't remember now whose suggestion the park was but the walk itself was his idea. I thought it was a bit strange to want to go for a walk but my boyfriends before then had all been known to me so I didn't know much about dating. Neither did he, it turned out, but he was too nervous to go out for a meal. I was a bit nervous but it being during the day and outside somehow made it less awkward. Probably because we could walk side by side rather than having to look at each other across a table. He was nervous but we soon got chatting and we had a nice time.

He was slim and a bit taller than me but not tall tall, not much hair as it had receded a lot leaving him with a bit of very short hair around the edge, glasses and a face that was quite pinched with concentration a lot of the time but when he smiled his face lit up. He seemed kind and gentle. Most of all he was keen and my fragile ego so needed to feel wanted and he ticked enough boxes for a second date, then a third and we became an item quite quickly. He had a house but we spent most of our time together at my flat. He didn't move in but we spent quite a lot of time together.

I hated my job in Manchester by this time so when he applied for, and got, a promotion at work that would mean moving to Surrey, I went with him. When I announced my plan to leave, my Grandpa and oldest brother (who worked for my Grandpa) told me they were planning on opening a restaurant and small hotel in our home town and were hoping I'd be involved. It's something I'd liked the idea of doing for a long time and how typical for this to come up as I was leaving. I went to Surrey anyway but with the intention that if the restaurant project came off I would come back.

My boyfriend rented his house out and went to Surrey for a few weeks on his own at first while I served my notice at work. He lived in Guildford initially in a tiny studio flat. He finally had a company car and was loving it but was lonely during the week. He'd come back at weekends or I'd go to Guildford. When I moved down we rented a bigger flat in Woking. The flat was in a purpose-built block and it had a nice little balcony overlooking the communal gardens. I'd lived with two of my previous boyfriends before, on a temporary basis in their homes either during the university holidays or before going travelling to Australia, but this was the first time I was moving in with my boyfriend to actually live together. I'd spent time with the others in their places but I always had the next thing coming (the next university year, next course, job) so it was only for a short time and it was a much better alternative for me than going back to my family home; that never seemed like a viable option. This was different. We were moving in together to start a life in a new place and we had a lovely flat to start that journey together.

Nearly every wall in the flat was papered with floral wallpaper and to make it look more like "ours" the landlord agreed to let us paint the wallpaper. We spent ages choosing colours and then painting; making our little place look lovely. At least that's what I was doing. I was making us a nest and who knew what would happen. It was exciting and full of possibility. I was nervous and scared and full of anticipation. You know when you're a little girl and you think about getting married one day, I very much had princess-like ideas in my head that I would get married at 26 to a handsome prince who would make me feel safe and cherish me and we would live happily ever after. Moving in with him aged 28 had way more riding on it than he, and even I, realised.

He was out of his hometown for the first time, spreading his wings. He was nervous but enjoying it. I think having me with him made it easier; I had lived in a few different places, I was used to finding out about how things worked, I was more "worldly-wise" than he was which was probably part of the attraction and also what he needed to get him out of the life he was in when we met. He wanted to drink it all in, soak up the freedom, the anonymity of knowing no-one and having no-one report back to his parents. I, on the other hand, wanted a soul mate, someone to take away my pain and to love and cherish me. Our relationship fell short for both of us.

I went back to work in London at the firm I used to work for. I just did it, it seemed the obvious thing to do. I think the flat was quite expensive but I don't remember looking for a job in Woking or Guildford. It was an easy option to go back to what I knew I suppose, comfort in the familiarity when I was embarking on this new stage of our relationship. I was supporting my boyfriend in his career progression without any thought of what I wanted. I commuted to the City every day and I hated it. I hated being at the mercy of the trains; if I missed one, it seemed like ages sometimes waiting for the next one after a miserable day at work. I hated the crowds of people. I hated the job. I went back to the same firm but to a different team and I worked for a man who had been there before but was now a partner and I didn't like him. He was aloof and not very approachable. I had been qualified for nearly 4 years by now so I knew much more and needed his input less, but there were still times I needed guidance and it was hard to gauge the right time. I have an innate ability to read a situation quickly and if it's not the right time then I wouldn't disturb someone. If I'd been less in tune, I would just have marched in, got what I needed and left. As it was, my sensitivity meant I agonised much more and I didn't like that environment. Law firms, on the whole, particularly large commercial firms are not easy places for sensitive people. I didn't recognise my sensitivity then, I saw it as yet another example of how I failed to fit in.

My boyfriend and I had lots of rows during our time in Woking. In the few photos I have of that time I can see the strain in both our eyes. I came from a family where shouting and screaming was the norm and he came from a family where silence was the norm so neither of us had the slightest idea how to live with another person, air our grievances constructively and resolve the conflict between us in a loving and respectful way. The resentment towards each other was palpable at times; we weren't giving each other what we needed. Amidst all this, we went to the wedding of a friend of mine. It was a lovely day, the reception was in a marquee at her parent's home and in a heady, drunken moment we ended up engaged!

My recollection is I suggested it would be nice if we got married and there was probably some persuasion on my part because I desperately wanted it. He could have said no of course, either then or the day after or a week after but he didn't. It wasn't how I imagined getting engaged but it had happened and I was proper pleased.

Someone wanted to be with me enough to marry me. At least that was my interpretation of the situation.

I was over the moon. I wasn't on great terms with my Mum by now and we didn't speak much so I wrote to her to share my news and ask for the diamond ring I inherited from my godmother which my Mum had in the safe at home. The letter I got back told me she hoped I would be happy but she had sold my ring a while ago as she needed the money. That was a slap around the face that brought me to attention. I knew things weren't good and if she'd asked I would have let her sell it but to not ask and not tell me was another reminder, not that I needed one, of how little I mattered in that family. That's how it felt. It also made me feel that my relationship was the way out of that pit of despondency. It had to work; I'd show her that I mattered. I'd show my Mum that someone thought I was worthy of love and affection even if she didn't.

Very soon after the engagement, I was asked if I wanted to go back to the north west to work with my family on the restaurant project. I wanted to get out of the law and give it a go, so we talked about it and decided I would go. He would come back a bit later when he'd got his tenant out of his house and he'd sorted the job situation.

To get the job in my old law firm in London I had spoken to my old boss. I was clear that it wasn't long-term but with no recruitment agency fee to pay and they knew me, I was welcomed back. When I came to leave some 8 months later, my then boss was annoyed and didn't speak to me for the whole of my 3-month notice period. My old boss hadn't told him I was there temporarily or if she had, he'd forgotten. It was a rubbish end to a rubbish job.

When I got back to the north west, I had nowhere to live as the plan was to move into my boyfriend's house (I know he was my fiancé by now but for some reason I don't like that word). I lived with a friend of mine in her spare room for a few weeks and when she moved I ended up living in my Grandpa's caravan for 7 weeks. It was parked up in the corner of a canal boat marina on the Leeds-Liverpool canal that Grandpa owned and my brother ran. The caravan was tiny but I liked it. It was easy to look after and it was my own little space. My boyfriend came back at weekends and we had 2 weeks in the caravan together when he moved back but it was a relief when his tenant left and we could move into the house.

I don't think he wanted to stay in Surrey without me. I don't remember putting pressure on him to come back and I don't recall a conversation about him staying longer, but he was angry. He had to go back to his old job, the company car went and he was back driving a van. He definitely liked living away and he probably held me responsible for spoiling his dream. In a strange twist, after years of doing what others wanted of me, I was doing what I wanted by moving back to work with my family. I felt guilty about ending his time away but excited to start this new chapter. We were engaged now and we were doing this together. It felt good.

His house was a typical terraced house, front door straight onto the pavement and a tiny courtyard garden. It had 2 bedrooms and a nice open plan living space and kitchen downstairs. He had owned it for years but never decorated it and it was pretty dingy, not because it had been rented out but more because it hadn't been shown any love. I wanted to make it a nice space for us so persuaded him to decorate. We got a decorator and chose lots of bright colours. We had new flooring downstairs and painted the floorboards upstairs. It was a bit over the top colour-wise by today's standards but this was the 90s. Clashing colours on the walls and the paintwork was all the rage.

I put my heart and soul into making that little house nice for us. I painted the courtyard walls and planted lots of pots to make it pretty. I was coaxing the house back into life, nurturing it as a safe space for us after my long days at work and his days at a job he didn't like. I was giving the house, his house, the love I thought it needed as a way of showing him love, my commitment and my gratitude for the chance to follow my dream. The garden would grow and flourish and be a nice space to "be" in. Doing was the only way I knew how to communicate. I was very busy "doing", at home and work. Having taken this leap, I wanted it to work. Perhaps if I had done less I might have given myself a chance to see more.

I was working on getting the restaurant and hotel ready for opening. I was loving sourcing everything we needed, choosing the décor, the uniforms, the glasses, the cutlery, the bed linen. My brother chose some things as well but the bigger picture of what the restaurant would look like was mine and I loved seeing it come together. I pretty much had no budget although I didn't go mad and to see something I had imagined come together was a real labour of love. I was giving that space my all as well, nurturing it into life. I couldn't wait to see it full of people and see them enjoying it knowing I had put it together. Knowing I had done something good. It was going to make me feel good about myself. It was going to be a happy beginning for something beautiful and it would give me a sense of pride.

In September 1998 the doors opened for the first time. It was mad. I have worked hard in the past but this was nothing I had ever known. I worked 6 days a week 7.30am to about 7pm, sometimes later. I was on call on

Sundays too. There was a head chef, a restaurant manager and I was the general manager. I had no industry experience and I had a lot to learn. My brother had other things going on elsewhere so I rarely saw him and I felt pretty alone most of the time. The restaurant manager and chef knew I was family so were wary of me. I was keen to keep a professional distance and I was massively out of my depth. It was a steep learning curve.

I liked the buzz at first but it wore off pretty quick and I wondered what the hell I'd taken on. I hated being on call 24/7, we weren't making much money, I thought the restaurant manager was up to no good but I didn't want to confront him. I couldn't do his job so if he left we'd be stuck. He had the gift of the gab too so would probably squirm his way out of it. Within 4 months my dream was all but gone and I was clinging on for dear life. The panic I felt as I saw what was becoming of my hopes and expectations was hard and the guilt I felt at not being able to fix it was like a weight pressing on my chest making it hard to breathe. Outside I might have looked like I was coping but inside was a very different story.

I couldn't talk to anyone about it either. To tell anyone how hard it was, how I couldn't cope and I just wanted to run away seemed churlish after the opportunity I had been given. I also knew they'd tell me to talk to my brother and Grandpa and I couldn't face that. I'd always steered my own path, always looked after myself, always made sure not to bother anyone. I was known as the clever one, the capable one, the safe pair of hands. If I admitted that I was struggling or just didn't want to do it anymore, where did that leave me? I just kept my head down and ploughed on instead of taking time to listen to my gut, take stock and decide what to do. I didn't feel like I had a choice.

On the plus side, the long hours at work gave me very little time to see my relationship was failing. I knew it but I couldn't face it and just hoped it would be ok. I wanted to be loved, feel like I was lovable, be cherished and mainly I wanted to be rescued. I wanted my boyfriend to say that our relationship was more important than the hours at the restaurant, that he could see what it was doing to me and that I could leave if I wanted and he would be there to look after me. Most of all, though, I wanted him to talk about setting a date for the wedding. He wouldn't. It was that Catch-22 – I wanted him to set a date to show he loved me and he wanted me to show I loved him before he'd talk about dates. During this time, I also began to realise he had a drink problem. We had always drunk alcohol together and sometimes we'd get drunk, very drunk. Hence the engagement. I had never thought it was a problem though. As our relationship got worse he drank more and more at home after work and I often left him asleep on the sofa to find him still there in the morning.

I began to hear about his drinking before he met me. How a litre bottle of strong vodka on Friday and Saturday nights used to be the norm and sometimes during the week. I was in a spiral of a failing job and a failing relationship and the darkness was closing in fast. I was trying hard to keep going at work and to cling on to the hope that there was a way back at home, but I also knew in my heart that it was done. All of it. I thought it couldn't get any worse.

The night of my 30th birthday celebration it

all came crashing down. My birthday itself was a Wednesday and the staff had made me breakfast with toast in the shape of a 3 and a 0. Their kindness made me cry. At home I barely got a "Happy Birthday" as I left for work at 7am and I had no idea what I'd go home to. I still can't remember what the rest of the day was like. On the Friday following my birthday a few friends came to the restaurant for dinner and were staying in the rooms. I was proud to show them the place and it was some of my oldest and dearest friends. All night I was on edge, partly because I was in my work place and I wanted to put on a good show for my guests and also the staff. I wanted my guests to be impressed and the staff to think how lovely all my friends were. It really mattered to me that it went well. My boyfriend barely spoke to me but was having a great time with my friends. I felt a dangerous cocktail of emotions – anger, jealousy and despair. Part of me hated him too that night but I think I hated myself more for feeling that hate.

I was sitting at the head of the table, I was the birthday girl after all, but I couldn't hide sitting in that place. I talked to my friends as best I could whilst watching what he was up to. I saw how much he drank and was scared to death of what he might say. I didn't want it to come out that night that I was a terrible girlfriend and he was going to leave me. I couldn't bear to be told I wasn't good enough in front of my friends. The desperation made my palms sweat and my heart beat fast. I couldn't concentrate. When the evening was finally over and we went to our room I let rip. I screamed at him and cried hysterically; I was beside myself with rage and despair. I was a mess. He said very little in return just that it was over. Of course it was but the realisation that everything I feared was coming true was too much to take. The lowest point was when somehow he ended up on the ground and I was astride him pummelling his chest out of sheer frustration demanding to know how he could do that to me. It was totally out of character and it was like time stood still somehow. A part of me stepped away from my body and looked over at where I was doing this to this man and whilst I couldn't believe I was doing it I could see that I was. I was numb to it, though, and as I watched I didn't feel remorse or pain or anything. Nothing. It felt like ages but it was probably only a minute or two until he pushed me off, got up and walked out. I heard his car start up and he left. It was over.

At breakfast I made some excuse about needing to get home, wished them all a safe trip home and left before anyone could ask any questions.

I was mortified and scared about what would happen next. He wasn't there when I got home so I busied myself with mindless jobs until he came home. I expected him to be drunk but he wasn't. I don't remember the conversation but that night I slept in the spare room and I stayed there for 3 months while I sorted out what I was going to do. It had been my home but it was his house and I'd always known that if we split up I'd have to leave. I thought we could be adult about it and get by; it was bearable for the first week or so but 3 months was just too long.

During that time, I realised that I was so unhappy at the restaurant I was going to leave, not without a sense of regret, but feeling like I had no other option. I looked for a legal job and quickly found one working in the legal department of the local council. The money was low compared to my other legal jobs but it was way better than at the restaurant so I took it.

When I was a lawyer I'd always wondered what it was like working in the legal department of a local authority and not in a law firm (working in a law firm is called private practice). I told my family I had a job and I was leaving. My brother said he appreciated that I'd been left with no support, which hadn't been the idea when I started, but events elsewhere had taken their attention. I felt relieved when the lack of support was acknowledged. I told them I realised what the problems were but I wasn't able to solve them. I was gutted it ended like that. I felt like a failure. I'd always wanted to run a restaurant but my idea was a little bistro type place, not 100 covers and a ten-bedroom hotel. Still, I knew I'd tried very hard; I'd worked myself into the ground and had nothing left to give. Maybe now, with age and the benefit of hindsight, I could have dealt with it very differently but I didn't know how to then. I only knew how to work hard and move on when I needed to. I had done that a few times by then and I knew how to do that. I had succeeded at most things in my life but

I couldn't do this anymore. I didn't want to if I was honest; working with my family had not been the happy, supportive environment I thought it would be. I was disappointed, I felt like a failure, and I crept away to lick my wounds.

I worked hard at the Council job. One day a colleague told me to stop working so hard as I was showing them up. That makes me laugh so much when I think about it. I can be like a robot sometimes, head down and plough my way through tons of work. It helps suppress feelings to keep busy and I was a master at that. The funny thing is I wasn't working that hard at the Council job, well not as hard as I had worked before and would work in the future. Writing all this down is making me see how many opportunities I had to take on board lessons, and I ignored them all. The "slow down" lesson, the "ask for help" lesson, the "you are doing great" lesson, the "this relationship is not good for you" lesson.

My time at the Council came to an end after a few months when I decided I needed more money if I was going to live by myself again and I got a job in private practice in a firm in South Manchester. This time I lived closer and didn't have such a big commute. The firm was a smaller one and the team was nice. There was nothing very special about that job, but one thing I remember is that the business manager told me after I started that most people go to the interview and say they are ambitious, will work hard, will do all the marketing asked of them and so on, but I said I know I can do the job, I will work hard but I won't do any marketing. By that, I meant pressing the flesh at events, making myself known in the town and trying to get new business. I've always hated all that stuff, and I decided the time had come to say I know it's expected but I won't do it. I'm actually quite good at it but I hate it. It just seems so false. As I got more senior, it became more expected, so I wanted to be clear from the outset. The business manager said they hired me anyway as they liked my honesty and that was a lesson I did take on board – be yourself, be honest. At every interview since then, I have just been me and been honest and I have not always got the job but if I did, I knew I got it based on the real me. The armour was still well and truly in place but I was learning to be true to myself in some situations. I wasn't aware that is what I was learning because if I had been, I would also have been aware that there were other situations where I wasn't true to myself.

CHAPTER 16

Whilst in London at age 25, I was diagnosed with PCOS (Polycystic Ovary Syndrome) and was advised that I shouldn't leave it too late to try for children as there was no way of knowing if and how it would affect my fertility. I wasn't too bothered at 25, but single again at 30, it started to bother me. I had never really thought of myself as maternal - having 2 younger brothers that I had been a second mum to had taken the novelty of that away - but when I thought I might not be able to have them, it made me realise that I didn't want a life without having children. It's common, isn't it, to only realise what we want when we can't have it.

My ex-fiancé was a lost soul and grew up with a very dominant father. There was a very dark side to him that I hadn't seen, or perhaps I had been blind to. I was so unaware of my own "stuff" I couldn't see anyone else's. I just wanted to be loved and kept safe but ended up with men who couldn't or didn't do that. There was a lesson to be learned there and I kept missing it. The lesson I failed to learn until a lot later was not to look externally for love and safety; to find it in and for myself first and then find it in a relationship. Now I know that if a situation keeps presenting itself to me, albeit in different ways and via different people, it's because there is a lesson there for me that I haven't learned yet. I was a latecomer to personal development, which is no surprise given the start I had, but it meant I was vulnerable to being hurt, let down, and worse. I genuinely have no idea how I kept bouncing back and hoping for better next time. A triumph of hope over experience, I think, is all I can say about that.

When I moved to South Manchester to start my new job, I moved to a nice little one bed flat and I decided things were going to get better. I liked living alone in my attic flat. You came in through the house front door, up two flights of stairs and then you came to a much narrower and steeper set of stairs that just led to my flat. It was cosy and quirky and I loved it. I liked the peace and quiet, I liked it being tidy and no-one else came in and messed it up but I was lonely too.

I don't recall how it came about but I was back in communication with Ayers Rock Guy. We'd always been on good terms and he's the only boyfriend I've ever managed to maintain a friendship with afterwards. I always had a soft spot for him, he was a thoroughly decent, reliable guy who liked me. He never made me feel jealous or inadequate, in fact he made me feel special and that was something I didn't feel very often. I also felt safe with him. Safe to be me and safe in that he would look out for me. We got together on and off over the years so I suppose it wasn't a massive surprise I reached out to him again in 1999 when I was hurting. I needed to be wanted, to feel that I wasn't totally worthless and most of all I needed to feel safe. In he drove in his trusty automatic Nissan Micra to save me – who needs a white horse?!!

He lived in Essex by now so it wasn't exactly a convenient rekindling but he found a training course in Manchester to get himself booked onto that also coincided with a football match at Maine Road (he's a lifelong footy fan). Perfect. I met a very old family friend of his there too. It felt nice. We played boyfriend and girlfriend for a weekend which gave my ego the boost it needed and gave us both the idea that maybe this time our timing would be right. After my split from the previous guy it was so fabulous to be adored again, to be with a tall, strong guy who made me feel safe and looked after. I forgot the reasons why it hadn't worked in the past and threw myself into "us" again.

I went down to his place in Essex one weekend and just as I arrived, so did he after drinks at work, a little bit drunk and his inhibitions low, declaring that he felt like the luckiest man alive that I was waiting on his doorstep and he had always loved me. It was everything I wanted to hear and I thought my heart was going to burst. Here was a great guy telling me he loved me; maybe I am lovable after all. Even then I had that foreboding feeling, that lurch in the pit of my stomach that this wasn't going to go right. I did my best to ignore it and we had a lovely weekend together.

He invited me to spend New Year's Eve with him at a party at his sister's house. Eek. Meeting his mum and sister again, that was another step. I felt really nervous. They were a very close family and his role didn't lend itself easily to supporting a fragile and needy girlfriend. I went to the party and as soon as we got there he was whisked off by his young niece who was very clearly staking her claim. I don't blame her at all. The party was great and his brother in law was a DJ with great taste in soul music so I did a lot of dancing that night. I didn't see him that much and I couldn't even find him at midnight to say "Happy New Year". It was the turn of the millennium and the only person I knew at the party was nowhere to be seen.

I knew then it wasn't going any further. It was bittersweet as I so wanted the safety he represented but I just knew I couldn't be part of his family. His connection with his family was a beautiful thing but there wasn't a Philippa-shaped hole for me to fit into as far as I could see. Coming so far down the order of priority for so much of my life had led me to a lonely corner of wanting to be by myself rather than not feel like I mattered. We met again a couple of times after that but it fizzled out. He had feelings for me and me him, but it wasn't enough to cope with what was going on for us both. The split was inevitable but he just didn't call. We never talked about it, worked it through, accepted it together. It just ended. Perhaps he was hurting too, I suppose I didn't call either. It was what it was.

I fell into a depression of sorts at this stage. I could just about make it to work and get through the day but I spent every evening and weekend on my own just moping around. Very Bridget Jonesesque. I was desperately lonely.

It was in this dire state of loneliness that I reconnected with the guy I used to be engaged to. I have no idea what I thought was happening and we only saw each other a few times. We went on a weekend away to the Lake District in a pretend world of make believe relationship. It was very weird but it made me feel wanted for a day or two. I was devastated a few weeks later to discover I was pregnant. We hadn't tried to conceive when we were together, but we hadn't taken precautions as we were happy to conceive, but nothing had happened. I was actually convinced that with my PCOS I couldn't conceive.

The PCOS weighed heavily on my mind by now and I seriously thought about having the baby. I would have no support from my family even though they lived quite close and he wanted me to have the baby but he didn't want to be with me. His friend had a child he saw occasionally so he thought that would work for him. I agonised for weeks over such a big decision whilst at the same time feeling like it wasn't really happening. I couldn't get my head round it. I wanted a baby, I didn't want to not have this baby but I couldn't see how I could bring this baby into the situation I was in. I was barely having a life myself and had no idea how I could support a child as well. I also knew this might be the one shot I had at having a baby and it was an incredibly hard decision to make.

I didn't have the baby and I told virtually no-one about it. A friend picked me up after the procedure and took me home and a couple of others had to know for other reasons but otherwise I kept it to myself. There was so much shame as well as sadness in that situation for me. I feel I made the best decision I could at the time with what I had available to me. I do sometimes think about it and feel the sadness. That boy or girl would have been 21 now. It still brings tears to my eyes. It was an awful time and I never would have imagined I would terminate a pregnancy. It made me question my own ignorance and I decided to make a concerted effort going forward not to judge people's decisions as we never truly know what we would do until we are in a situation.

At the same time as this was happening, I'd landed my dream job working as an in-house property lawyer in a company in Manchester. I was fed up with working in private practice and wanted to work for a company instead. I was also trying a dating website as I'm a great believer in taking action; if I want to meet someone, I don't expect it to just happen. I also think it's a good way of meeting new people and even if you don't find true love directly you might find it via one of the people you meet.

I got on well with this one guy by email, but when I met him he turned out to be an ex-heroin addict turned vicar (I kid you not) who wanted to counsel me on my shortcomings (his words). No second date there. Then there was the guy who I stupidly gave my address to and he picked me up in his Porsche and then sped down the road and onto the motorway at 90mph. I seriously thought I was in trouble. I was petrified but tried not to show it as I had no idea where we were and how to get home from the country pub we'd ended up at. It turned out he was a knob who was trying to impress me with his car and driving and wanted to see me again. Err, no thanks. The third guy I met was gentle and kind and thought I was fabulous, so naturally, that didn't last.

So I am working my 3 months' notice in the south Manchester law firm before moving to my fab new job as an in-house lawyer, and I am dating the guy who thinks I am fabulous just after terminating the pregnancy. All of these dates were just dinner and drinks. Nothing physical because I couldn't even think about that after the pregnancy. I knew it wasn't going anywhere with the nice guy but I agreed to go to his Christmas party with him. Then something terrible happened to one of his friends and he wanted to take a break to concentrate on what had happened, which was fine with me, but he still wanted me to go to the party. I did go, but he left early as he was so upset about his friend's accident.

I ended up chatting to a guy at the party

who was from out of town and I had the most amazing time with him. This guy was attentive, interesting and interested. I told him almost my entire life story and he told me some of his and how he had just met the girl of his dreams. I thought I would never see him again and it was good to talk about all the things that had been whirring around my head for months. He was already with someone, the girl of his dreams, so I was on safe territory. We talked until 4am and it felt like a dream.

Before I left, he told me that I was the girl of his dreams and he'd meant me when he said that earlier. I don't think he played me, but I could have been wrong. Anyway, if he did, he got more than he bargained for! We exchanged contact details, and when I fell out with my Mum a couple of days later on Christmas Eve, I ended up spending Christmas with him at his brother's and having the most fabulous time.

6 weeks later, I'd left my fab new job (I'd only been there 3 weeks) and moved to Bristol to live with him. I was happy to leave the north west after what had happened over the previous few months and I believed a fresh start was what I needed. I was, of

course, running away again but I believed I was running to something special this time.

There was a dark side to him, too. We drank a lot at the beginning, but once I got a job, the drinking had to slow right down for me and I was then accused of being boring. He liked that I was a lawyer but couldn't seem to get that I couldn't hold down a job like that and drink as we did at the beginning all the time. Now, I think it highlighted his reliance on alcohol when I backed off and he didn't like it. No-one wants a mirror held up to them to see their self-destructive habits in all their glory but he clung on to his drinking for all he could and it slowly but surely drove us apart. Not the drinking *per se*, but I didn't behave well around the drinking and tried to get him to stop or slow down at least. I was so sure we were going to "fix" each other, how could it be anything else after the romantic way it started? I thought we'd live happily ever after but I knew that couldn't be the case if he drank so much. I thought if I smothered him with love he would give up the drink. Nope. It just made him pull away which made me cling on more until he yelled at me that I was too needy for him and it was over.

I have hated the word needy ever since. It is so accusatory and has so much judgement attached to it. Yes, I had, and have, needs that had never been attended to, ever, but that didn't make me a bad person. The relationship was destroying us both, not fixing us, and he ended it as his friend told him he was screwing me up, and I didn't deserve that. I pleaded with him not to listen to his friend; that it would work out. Thank god he would have none of it, although I was heartbroken at the time.

Putting all this down in print, I can see all the lessons and opportunities to heal I missed along the way, but I was still trying to survive. The relationship with him, in particular the drinking, triggered the trauma from being at home with my Mum. Thank goodness I had that survival streak in me.

CHAPTER 17

Like many big moments in my life, a few things came together to finalise my decision to try and find my Dad. Find him, hopefully, but I had no idea how it would go. I didn't know how he would react. I wasn't even sure he was alive. What I did know was that I couldn't put it off any longer. It had been about 20 years of desperately wanting to know stuff and that was a big hole to fill. I had that deep feeling of guilt, too, that partly drove me on.

It was the year 2000. New Year's Eve 1999 was a night that had been talked about for years – Prince had sung about it, so had Pulp, in fact the turn of the century had loomed large for pretty much a lot of the 90s. Many people were concerned about the millennium bug that was going to blow up technology as the year turned to 2000. It didn't. The pressure to do something amazing on New Year's Eve 1999 had grown steadily to the point where people were spending thousands of pounds on big parties, fireworks, boat trips, you name it. I, on the other hand, started the year splitting up with Ayers Rock Guy, still in a mess about what had happened during 1999, I had a job I didn't like that much and I often spent weekends totally on my own. It felt like I was failing at life somehow. I was miserable.

The start of the new century made me think of the passing of the old century, new beginnings and a bit of "if not now, then when?". I was single and just turned 31 which gave me a massive jolt of reality; I had well and truly left my 20s and I couldn't stop life moving on. The events of 1999 were still haunting me. My Mum's relationship with my Step-Dad was in a desperately bad place and I realised that asking my Mum about my Dad probably wasn't going to make things any worse. Those were my main concerns at the time but a little part of me also just wanted to do it now because I'd put it off for long enough in case it was hard for other people; it was hard for me not knowing about my Dad, not knowing what happened, why it happened, just not really knowing anything. Time was passing so quickly and the need to find out more about my Dad became all consuming. I felt so disconnected from my family, so much of a misfit that I needed to know if my Dad was the reason why. Did he have anything for me that could ease my fear and pain? I had been abandoned by him already so I knew there was a real risk he would reject me or not be who I desperately needed him to be but the yearning to be part of something, be accepted, was so intense I had to take that risk.

When we saw our Dad as children, me and my brother usually saw him at his mum's house, our lovely Grandma, which was familiar and a safe place to be but I always knew it was odd that we didn't get to go to his house, wherever that was. I sort of always knew we were on borrowed time. I must have known that living with my Dad wasn't an option although I don't remember ever speaking about it. I just somehow knew and I was right. My Dad was gay and whilst it was no longer illegal to be openly gay there was still very much a stigma attached to it and that was used by my Mum and Step-Dad (backed by my Grandpa) to persuade my Dad to stay away. My Grandpa was a wealthy man and he told my Dad that if he stayed away from us (me and my brother) then he would make sure we were all right. By that my Grandpa meant financially all right and he did what he said he would but the cost to me in missing those years with my Dad was not worth the price.

At school I was in a group of five friends and one of the others had divorced parents. She didn't see her dad either but on her 18th birthday her Dad re-appeared and with my birthday only a few months later I longed for the same. Even though I had no idea where he was, I knew he'd know it was my birthday and I had a little seed of hope. I didn't tell a soul. He didn't get in touch.

I had a party and lots of family and friends came. To top it off, my Mum booked a stripper and with friends and family there it was awful. I was embarrassed and it ruined what was supposed to be a celebration of me becoming an adult. Unbeknown to me, my Dad owned a taxi company nearby and for that WHOLE evening had been sending taxis to my party to take people home. Later I found out he was as heartbroken as I was.

I had a wild 3 years living in London. I was earning good money, I had a good job and I was living in a flat with fun girls in Clapham, a nice part of south west London. I had no-one to answer to, I was free to come and go as I pleased, free to spend my money as I pleased and I had no more exams to do. It was like finally becoming an adult and really living. It was freedom like I had never experienced before and whilst I loved it for a time it began to feel quite pointless. I also began to feel I had no idea what life was supposed to be about.

I wasn't playing at happy couples like I was before I went to Australia, I was single and lapping up all the fabulous things living in London had to give. Even going to work on the smelly, crowded Northern Line was fun at the beginning but that novelty soon wore off. I hated the tube and I was so hot and bothered by the time I'd walked to the tube that forcing myself onto a crowded train with my nose stuck in someone's arm pit for 30 minutes was not something I could bear for long. I had inherited my Gran's car when I was 21. It was an original 1972 burnt orange MGB GT and I had it in London with me. I discovered that there was a car park just on the south side of Tower Bridge and my office was just on the north side of Tower Bridge so I started driving to work. I was stuck in traffic but it was so worth not being on the tube that I didn't care. Environmental concerns weren't such a thing back then. Obviously I wouldn't do that now!

I walked up from the car park and over the bridge every morning and I loved that walk. Tower Bridge is beautiful. It is one of the most famous of the bridges over the River Thames. It is magnificent and always made me smile every day I walked over it. On days I was late, and the bridge was lifting so I had to wait, I wasn't always so impressed but that was hardly the bridge's fault. Tower Bridge isn't to be confused with London Bridge which is the next bridge along the River Thames going west. Tower Bridge is by far the more impressive. Tourist buses flocked over the bridge as did tourists but when I was on my way to work it wasn't too busy and I could walk across in quiet contemplation of the day ahead. It was quite a way to start the day.

Tower Bridge is a bascule (drawbridge) and suspension bridge with two Victorian Gothic style towers that are connected with two walkways (one at road level and one much higher) to resist the horizontal forces from the suspended parts at either end of the bridge. The towers are made of stone and the huge chains and rods of the suspension parts of the bridge are painted white and turquoise. The bridge is huge and imposing, more so because it is not that long. The imposing towers seem to leer down as though daring vehicles and people to cross. The drawbridge in the middle opens occasionally and just knowing it is capable of that gives it a menacing feel as though it could open up and swallow you at any moment. That is one way to look at the bridge but I didn't see it like that. It is a famous landmark and I was excited to cross that bridge most days, as though I was entering a new world full of potential and excitement. Just over the bridge on the north side is the Tower of London. I couldn't believe I was working in the great metropolis of London let alone overlooking the Tower of London. I was definitely caught up in the excitement of that and even when the shine of the job rubbed off I still loved looking at the

Tower of London and Tower Bridge.

Driving to work in London was an odd thing to do though. My friends all thought it was a strange thing to do. I didn't care. No-one could stop me and I was doing things my way. For once in my life I was being and doing what I wanted. Well the "being" was limited by what I allowed myself to be out in the world; the real me, the anxiety ridden, unworthy, devoid of confidence me surfaced when I was alone but in company I could put on quite a good show of appearing to have it together. The conditioning was strong. I am my mother's daughter after all.

If the weather was nice, at weekends we'd go to the pubs by the river in Richmond and have a fabulous time getting very drunk. I later found out that at that same time my Dad was running a pub just 10 minutes' walk away from the river. He was so close and I didn't know. I sometimes wondered what would have happened if I'd bumped into him on the street. Would I have recognised him? Would I have felt I knew him? I look very like my Mum and my brother looks very like him so there might have been a flicker of recognition. I think he knew I was living in London through contact with my Mum so he might have had more than a flicker. I doubt he would have acted on it even if he had and I'm pretty sure I wouldn't have either. I might have felt unsettled but I doubt I would have had the nerve to say anything. It's the fairytale princess ending desire in me to dream that we would have seen each other in the street, our eyes would meet and he would tell me how beautiful I am and how proud he is of me and how sorry he was that he abandoned me. The reality is that even if I had bumped into him I would probably have literally bumped into him, after too much to drink, and mumbled sorry and run off giggling with my friends.

It seems so unbelievable now what happened when I was a child and that anyone could have thought I was better off not knowing him, but time has worked its magic and I can accept that, whilst I don't understand it, I think they thought I was better off not knowing.

In 2000, even though I had decided I would try and find him, like the bloody "good girl" I was, I also decided I had to tell my Mum first. That was the right thing to do. That's what they did in books and films so it must be the right thing. I had no real-life reference of the right thing, never have had, so I took my cues from fiction. I also felt the notion that I somehow owed her an explanation before I took the action.

It was a cold February day when I drove over to her house feeling extremely nervous. It was only 22 miles but it seemed so far that day. The distance also passed by much quicker than I wanted. I would stop and hesitate at every junction, hope the traffic lights would turn red and hold me there for ages, anything to delay actually telling my Mum. I kept my distance from her a lot of the time. My youngest brothers were both at university so with no kids at home her drinking escalated and I never knew what state she would be in when I got there. She was rattling around in the house we had all lived in, on her own since the split from my Step-Dad and afraid she would be forced out of the house. I had no empathy for her situation at the time but now, writing this, I feel so sad for how things were for her at that time. It must have been awful and I hope she had friends to talk to about it.

I knew that if I stood any chance of getting

her in a good mood I had to go early before she got stuck into the drink so I rocked up at her house mid-morning. I'd told her I was coming but she managed to act surprised. She did that all the time and I never knew if she genuinely forgot or did it on purpose to show she wasn't making an effort or anything. Either way it always left me feeling irrelevant. I had no idea how she was going to react so I started saying something about not wanting to hurt her and I just needed to know and she got so impatient she told me to just get on with it so I blurted out that I was going to try and find my Dad. Well that shut her up, momentarily. After all this time I think she'd thought I'd forgotten or something.

I expected her to go ballistic, but to my surprise the first thing she said was "He's gay you know". She was surprised to learn that I knew. Well I sort of knew. I don't think it had ever been said when we were younger but I remember he had a male friend with him sometimes when we saw him after they split up. Then one day at school when I was in the 6th form, a boy I knew and was sort of friends with sidled up to me and asked quietly if I knew my Dad was gay. I didn't even know he knew my Dad. I called my Step-Dad "dad" almost straight away, as I felt that was expected, so no-one even knew he wasn't my real dad as far as I was aware. I was so shocked by what the boy said that I just mumbled yes of course I knew and wandered off. I didn't know as such but it didn't come as a surprise. So some 15 years later when my Mum said that to me, it wasn't a surprise and frankly I didn't care. I told her I just wanted to know more about him and to my utter surprise she said she knew people who were still in touch with him and she gave me their address. Just like that. After all that time of hoping he'd come and find me, want to know me and giving up on that, here was the means to make that meeting happen for myself.

Thinking about it, I think my Mum was pretty scared about what might then happen but to her credit she made it very easy for me to find him. We had a difficult relationship, to say the least, but I am deeply grateful that she did that for me when she could have denied any knowledge of his whereabouts. I wonder what would have happened if I'd asked her earlier? Perhaps she thought I didn't want to know because I never asked? I'll never know so I don't give it much airtime but maybe if I'd been braver sooner it would have worked out all right.

Armed with an address I went back to my attic flat and I wrote a letter. I put pen to paper in my best handwriting (it's not the neatest!) and first of all I wrote a letter to the people whose address I had, asking them to pass the enclosed letter onto my Dad. Then I wrote a much longer letter to my Dad. I tell him that I know he's gay and I don't care. I tell him that Mum has just told me he had a triple heart bypass a few years earlier and she was about to tell us about it when it looked like he might die but he pulled through and she didn't tell us anything. I tell him that I just want to know him, see if we can have a relationship. I am full of hope as I write, that it might be a fairytale ending. My handsome prince of a father will come and scoop me up, make me feel loved and carry me off to happy ever after. I suppose I did have him on a pedestal. When life isn't all that happy as a child and something is missing from it, it's an easy go-to to believe that if whatever is missing reappears all will be right in the world. I wasn't aware of feeling that in so many words but now I see that I was.

There have been a series of "if only"s to cling onto throughout my life - if only my Dad had kept in touch, if only my Mum hadn't been an alcoholic, if only I hadn't been so fat, if only I had been prettier. I think that my Dad leaving left a big gaping whole inside that left me wide open to something else and unfortunately what I found to suck up was a whole lot of criticism, harshness and unkindness and I took it all to heart. It's only quite recently that I have appreciated how sensitive I must have been as a child to feel all this and not say anything. To know that I was hurting so much yet to also know that to voice it would cause pain for others and probably trouble for me that I kept it all in, buried deep inside me never to be let out.

I saw my Mum on a Saturday, wrote the letters on Sunday and posted them on Monday. I didn't tell anyone else about it; I didn't tell my Mum I'd written so quickly. In my head I was thinking maybe a week or so before I heard anything. He would need time to get the letter from his friends, take it all in and then maybe write back. All was calm just now as the time passed.

I was at my job in south Manchester. I was quite senior so I had an office of my own and on Wednesday morning the phone rang and I picked it up without thinking, probably deep in thought about whatever I'd just been looking at, and I said my name like I usually do but in response I hear my name repeated back to me followed by "it's your Dad". All I could say is "Oh my god", I think I said it 4 or 5 times, over and over. That's all I could get out at the time. I could hardly get my breath let alone string a sentence together. I'm not usually lost for words believe me! He explained that his friends had got the letter on Tuesday and rang him straight away. He'd asked them to open his letter and read it to him. They'd posted it to him and he'd got it that morning. He was absolutely over the moon that I had got in touch, he was blubbing a bit and saying he thought it would never happen and how happy he was. I was trying not to get too emotional as I was at work and the office walls were glass so everyone could see in. I was in shock. Exposed in my vulnerability by my Dad and exposed at work through the glass.

I had never had anyone so pleased to hear from me. It was such a special moment. He realised I was struggling to talk so we arranged to meet 10 days later. I would go down to London on the train and meet him. I was to book my train ticket and let him know the time and he'd meet me at Euston. I had to go for a walk round the block to get my breath back after that.

The train was going to arrive early. When are trains early? Here I am about to meet my Dad again after 20 years and, much as I have wanted this moment to happen for a long time, the train arriving early is almost more than I can bear. All my energy is being taken up by trying to stay calm; trying to stop my heart beating so loud I wonder if the whole carriage can hear it. Panic starts to set in as the train trundles into the station and I am shaking as I try to open the door. I step down on the platform and take a deep breath to calm my nerves. It's going to take more than a deep breath today. The reality of what is about to happen stops me in my tracks and the woman who got off behind me has to swerve to avoid walking into me. She tuts loudly as she passes by. Usually I would be apologising profusely but today my mind is on other things. I wrote the letter, had the phone call and made the arrangements for today but it is only now standing on the platform that I realise I might not recognise him. He sent me a photo but it was a few years old. Until now I have relied on this fantasy notion that I would step off the train and my Dad would be there standing on the platform to welcome me with open arms. The train being early has scuppered that and I am left wandering along the platform to the main hall scanning faces to see if I recognise anyone.

I have a picture of my oldest brother in my mind as he looks very like my Dad but still I find myself thinking a couple of times if this or that tall man with white hair is my Dad. I feel a bit stupid and the voice in my head starts telling me how ridiculous I am to have expected a magical reunion. Beautiful things like that don't happen to me. My heart is beating so fast it's rattling my ribcage, my legs are starting to feel like jelly and my breath is shallow and fast. I feel the urge to run away and I'm not sure how long I can do this. Then I see him. Instinct tells me without a shadow of doubt that it's him. It's strange looking at someone you hardly know and yet you recognise they have been in your heart forever. The sort of knowing that you only get from a place of belonging. This was my Dad and we belonged together. He looks over and sees me. I quickly walk over; I want to run but it seems so ungainly. He's quite tall and after an awkward second or two of the "to hug or not to hug" dance I find my face buried in his chest and I am crying like a baby. His baby. A tidal wave of emotions crashes over me and drowns me in tears. Although I don't really know him, it feels safe to cry and just let him hug me. We must have made quite a sight.

After a few minutes we go outside and sit down on a little concrete wall and gather ourselves together. I babble about the train being early, about not knowing if I'd recognise him, about how mad the whole thing is. Then we have a proper laugh about it. It's lunch time and he says he has booked a table in Covent Garden so off we go.

I remember walking into the fabulous place he has booked, dark and atmospheric, the lady takes our coats and when asked what we'd like to drink we answer in unison "Gin and Tonic please" and we laugh, probably in relief. At least we have one thing in common. I watch him talking and when he goes to scratch his left ear he doesn't do it with his left hand, he uses his right hand and stretches it in an arc over his head. My brother does the exact same thing. My heart is filling up bit by bit. We order lunch - we both order …. liver. I don't think I've ever been out when someone else has ordered liver too. We look at each other and laugh. We have another G&T and then he asks tentatively if I'd like to come and see his pub and meet his friends. I don't want it to end so of course I say yes. After all this time I'm not ready to let this wonderful reconnection end yet.

When we get there the excitement in the air is palpable. It turns out a lot of his staff and friends knew he was meeting me and they're all there waiting to see if I make an appearance. My Dad walks in first and then I follow and the place erupts. Well that's what it felt like but I suppose it wasn't quite as dramatic as that. Suddenly we're surrounded by people and my Dad is introducing me "This is my fabulous/clever/wonderful daughter Philippa. She's a lawyer you know. First in our family to go to university." He was so proud that night and so was I. It was a bit like a fairytale and recalling it now, it was like a dream. Until that point I had never once thought I was someone to be proud of. I'd only felt that I was in the way, having to be helpful to justify my existence. Over the course of the evening my Dad's friends came and spoke to me and whispered conspiratorially how happy they were that I had got in touch with him. They'd thought about getting in touch with me three years earlier for his 50th birthday but then they didn't. So many missed opportunities for us to reconnect over the years but at long last there I was. It was such a relief.

That night I discovered why I'd always felt like I didn't fit in at home. Why I felt different to everyone else. Why I found it hard to cope with. Why I liked change. Why I easily got bored. All those things I got from him and here with him I felt at home. That place in my heart and head that until now had been a dream where I felt safe, as though I belong, as though I am wanted. Comfy and cosy like a snuggly blanket on a cold day. I felt like I belonged to my Dad that day, as though I had support, he was finally there for me. Proud of me. So happy that I had looked for him and found him. Me and my Dad, together again. It was a BIG day.

He told me he always hoped me and/or my brother would look for him and he told himself that if we wanted to know him we would look. He didn't seem to understand, even then, that it works both ways. I thought that if he wanted to know me he would find me. That to not look for me left me lost in the wilderness of not belonging; it reaffirmed the abandonment.

It was a fabulous day but somewhat bittersweet too; all that wasted time. My friends arrived around midnight and I went back to stay at their place not very far away. I didn't want to leave the bubble I'd been in all day; I just wanted it to go on and on and on. Of course it had to end. I had a train back to Manchester the next day and I went back with a very happy heart and yet a slight trepidation at what would happen next.

I wanted to keep it as my secret for now but I knew I would tell my brother and probably my Mum and then some friends. The first person I told was my sister-in-law who told me she thought my brother would be ok about it. He was surprised and not quite as keen to meet him as I was. He was very angry I think although we never talked about it. I don't know what the overriding emotion was underneath his anger. We didn't talk about stuff at home so as adults we didn't have that skill. My Dad came up a few weeks later and met my brother. It was a bit frosty, I believe, but it went ok.

I also told my Mum so my Dad went to see her too. He told me he felt guilty about how things turned out for her. He married her just as he turned 21 which was only a year after homosexuality was decriminalised. Growing up he knew something was different for him but he didn't know what so he married my Mum hoping it would work out. My Grandpa took them out to a lot of nice restaurants and my Dad came to realise he was more interested in the waiters than my Mum. He was trapped and didn't know what to do. They got married, had me 13 months later and my brother 20 months after that. They got by but gradually they became more and more unhappy until they decided to split. There was a day, maybe 2 or 3 at the most as far as I recall, of heated discussions and arguing when I would sit at the top of the stairs hanging onto the banister listening and then one day we came home from school and the TV and stereo had gone along with my Dad. I couldn't understand why he'd take the TV and leave us without one.

He felt very guilty so now he had the chance to make it up to my Mum. He used to go and see her, buy her things and try to make up for the past. He spent time with my brother and his young family and he spent time with old friends and his brother's wife, my lovely auntie. My Dad's brother died suddenly in his 30s which was a real shock. My auntie remarried but stayed in my life and has always been a great support to me. She has been my connection to that side of my family which has been a great comfort over the years.

So the reunion seemed a success but I felt like I was left out again. I'd gone to the trouble of finding him and he spent most of his time with other people. The fairytale ending I had wanted was fading fast and I was distraught. I didn't begrudge other people getting time with him, as he ran a pub he would come up in the week when I was at work, but I felt like I'd just been the conduit to reconnect with people from his old life. I'd wanted to be a special part of it but I felt like an add on.

Now I can see that it was my fear of rejection that made me see it like that. I was looking for signs that I was surplus to requirements, signs to confirm what I already thought. Everywhere I looked I saw those signs and I drank them in like a G&T. I didn't just have a mask to disguise my emotions, I had a thick suit of armour that nothing was getting through which kept me safe of sorts but it meant nothing got in either. I was cold, lonely and hurting. One night my Dad came to my flat for dinner and it was during that evening that he told me about Grandpa telling him to leave us alone and he'd see that we were looked after. After we'd eaten I spent the evening showing him all my photo albums, all the things he missed, telling him all the stories behind the pictures. It must have been so hard for him hearing it all; so much pain. He told me he truly thought he was doing the right thing leaving us alone but could see how much we'd had to endure. I well and truly made him feel awful. And that is what I intended. I was bloody angry that I was being left out again so I was going to hurt him too. I regret that now as I think that set us back and if I hadn't done that maybe we would have got closer. On the other hand, I didn't know how to express my feelings and that was my clumsy way of expressing my anger and my Dad didn't know how to deal with it.

It was about 10 months after finding my Dad that I moved to Bristol after meeting the guy at the Christmas party. I was in so much pain. I wasn't running away from my Dad, he was still in London, I was running away from the other things that had happened up north and I felt I had no support. Despite several invites and promises, my Dad never came to Bristol preferring to spend his time off work with family and friends up north. It felt like another betrayal and yet again I didn't matter. It was another confirmation of my worthlessness. All hopes of the fairytale had well and truly dissipated.

I did continue to see my Dad. I stayed in his pub quite a few times. I still had friends in London and would meet them. My Dad was a workaholic so I worked all week, I would see him perhaps for an early dinner on a Saturday and then go out with friends while he worked. He would be working again on Sunday. If I didn't go to see him, I didn't see him. Me and my then boyfriend went for New Year's Eve one year and my Mum announced she was going too so I got bumped out of staying in the pub to the B&B across the road. My Dad did that to give me space from my Mum but it felt like we'd had to give way for her. As usual she was more important. On New Year's Day we all went out for a meal and Mum showed her true self by getting extremely drunk and being vile to me in front of everyone. I excused myself from the table and went to the toilet to have a cry and calm down. Actually, she did me a favour because until then I think my Dad and my then boyfriend thought I was exaggerating.

It felt a little bit that my reconnection with him was thwarted but with hindsight I see I was looking for him to somehow "fix" me. Not only was that a tall order for him after all that time, he would have had no idea as my suit of armour kept it all hidden. More importantly though I was still looking for something external to fix my problems.

In 2004 on Boxing Day I had a phone call to say my Dad had passed away. He was only 58 years old. He was found in his bed. After his triple heart bypass some years before, he hadn't managed to give up smoking even though heart disease had killed both his father and brother very young. A post mortem showed that he suffered a DVT, probably on a trip to Egypt earlier that year, and the clot broke up and hit his lungs in the night. Poor Dad. I was very stoic and I had no idea how to grieve for a man I didn't know that well. I sorted his flat out above the pub, his paperwork, his estate.

We had two funerals, one in London which was packed and the cremation up north. Luckily he had told me he wanted his ashes put with his family and he showed me where. So at least I knew that was the right thing to do. After the phone call, I had driven straight up to London with my then boyfriend. After going to the pub to see his staff and to take his papers from his office, my boyfriend drove me around south London that Boxing Day night looking at churches that looked like they might be suitable for the funeral. I had no idea. Luckily the church round the corner from the pub was fabulous, gay friendly and the vicar was amazing. I cried my eyes out all the way through the meeting with the vicar telling him the bits I knew about my Dad. I chose hymns and readings in a blur. The only hymns I could remember were ones from school. It felt so inadequate but I didn't know what else to do. I got an undertaker I knew up north to sort the cremation and he found an undertaker in London to help me and we had a fabulous celebration of his life in London then the day after a cremation up north.

I spoke at both ceremonies. I wanted to. I needed to. It was about expressing my feelings for him out loud as I wouldn't have the chance to say them to him. In London, the church was packed with his friends and I had chosen an over the top floral decoration for his coffin in green and pink and white. It was lovely and I think he would have liked it. He loved flowers, the more unusual the better.

People were dressed in colourful outfits. It was yet another out-of-body experience for me as I stood up to speak about someone who meant so much to me but I didn't know that well in front of a lot of people I didn't know at all. I felt like an outsider and a bit of a fraud yet I needed to speak. I started with "Too soon, too soon, those are the words that keep going round my head". It was too soon for him to be taken just 5 years after I found him again. I talked about the pain of growing up without him, the joy of finding him again and how sad I was that he was going to miss key moments like weddings and meeting his grandchildren. I think he would have been a brilliant granddad.

The pub where he worked when he died was just round the corner from the church and they put on the wake for him. I was angry with his area manager as they knew he worked all hours, too hard for someone with his health conditions and they let him do it. To be honest, they wouldn't have been able to stop him but I needed to blame someone so it was his area manager that got my Paddington-like stares and short replies to his questions that day.

The church service and wake felt like a

fitting tribute to him that day and it was so lovely to hear stories of how much he helped people and took care of them. He'd given money to people to help them fight to see their kids as he regretted not fighting for us. He lent people money whenever he could and one person tried to give me the money they had on them and promised to send me what else they still owed my Dad. I told them that the debt died with him and there was no need to give me any money. It's what he would have wanted. He was a truly kind and generous man. I am so lucky that I got 5 years with him, even if they were not quite what I wanted, but I wish I'd had more. We never know what is going to happen next.

The service up north the day after was at the crematorium. I adapted what I said to be shorter and I made sure I got in some barbed comments about how sad it was that he felt he had to leave and how much we missed having him around. How we didn't understand what happened and why he left. My Mum was at this service and just sat there pulling faces. She's had a drink beforehand, naturally, and the faces she pulled looked like she wanted to say it wasn't her fault. I don't know what she meant as I didn't ask. I just know that I felt she wanted it to be about her and she certainly wasn't supporting me and my brother in any way.

There was a group of people there who I didn't know and when I went to talk to them they told me they used to work for his taxi company. It had been a long time ago at this stage but they still had such lovely things to say about him and they told me he used to talk about me and my brother all the time. They all felt so sorry for him that he didn't get to see us. It was getting to be emotional overload at this stage but I managed to keep it together, just. We had a wake in a local pub and my brother and I went back to the crematorium later that day by ourselves to meet the undertaker to scatter the ashes. They had agreed to let us do it that day as we had come from London that morning and needed to go back that night. The ashes were still warm and as we poured them out together under the tree where his parents' and brother's ashes were scattered, I whispered goodbye and the wind carried some of the ashes away. Most of the ashes stayed in a heap and as it was early January it was cold and the steam coming off the ashes was like a final breath, a goodbye. It was so final. Death is like that, so bloody final. It was too soon.

He didn't have a house to sell or anything like that. After the funeral there was quite a bit of paperwork but that was it. I hadn't seen him very often but I'd known he was there and then he wasn't there anymore. I was so sad that he was gone, so young, and so much left unsaid. I consoled myself that 5 years was better than nothing and it was. Yes, had I known it was going to end so quickly I might have done things differently, but most of what I would have done differently is with the benefit of age and realising that he did the best he could with what he had available to him.

The most important thing I got from finding my Dad was a sense of belonging. Or at least that's what I thought but in reflection I think what happened for me in meeting my Dad was the start of healing the abandonment wound. I feel that this wound so young caused the foundations I had to crumble and this was the root of my feelings of unworthiness and "not enoughness". My Mum's drinking was always going to affect me, given the pivotal role she played in my life, but the lack of foundation allowed it to seep to so deep that I stood chest deep in the misery of it for so much of my life. I wish I had talked to someone about it much sooner, I wish I hadn't kept it bottled up, I wish I had known that I wasn't alone and had the courage to reach out for help.

I don't feel that my Mum is around anymore but I do feel the presence of my Dad and my Grandma and I feel they are watching over me, particularly my Grandma. In late 2020 I heard an interview with a woman who works with people and their Akashic records. It sounded intriguing and something drove me to book a session with her. My understanding of the Akashic records is that every person has a record that holds everything that has ever happened and will happen to them, in previous lives, in this life and in future lives. The records include all thoughts, feelings, emotions and intentions. In my session my Dad appeared and led me to the records where my Grandma appeared as my guide in the records. It was a fascinating session and the main thing I took from it was saying goodbye to my Mum. It was extremely emotional.

I have a few old photos from when I was little and I have looked at them many times. The last time I looked at them was after the Akashic records session. In the pile I found a photo that I don't remember ever seeing before, it certainly hadn't registered before. The photo is of me as a baby, probably 6 months old or so, being held by my Grandma standing up on her knee and it looks like we are both shouting the same thing, as though we are both saying loudly something like "yeah". We both look very happy. The photo is now in a frame in my office and looks down at me as I write.

My Dad was a lovely man and I will always remember him with a lot of love. I feel he is watching over me, with his mum, my Grandma, making sure I'm doing ok. It's a comfort but still a sense of sadness and, perhaps, a sense of such precious time wasted.

CHAPTER 18

I am 33, my relationship has ended and I am heartbroken. When things like this happen I usually run away but for some reason I don't this time and I stay in Bristol. My old friend from university has a spare room and he kindly agrees to put me up for a few months. His flat is in a nice part of Bristol by the docks and I would spend quiet evenings after work on his little balcony wondering what to do next. I don't think I ever thought about leaving Bristol. I liked where he lived and a flat in the next block came up for rent but I just missed out on it. I was disappointed but that's what happens. Rather than allow myself to feel the feelings, I distracted myself by jumping onto a dating website, two websites in fact, and started having email conversations with what sounded like nice men.

One night in November 2002, I met up with one of them in a big faceless chain-type pub on the outskirts of Bristol. I'd said I wanted to meet somewhere big and open, just in case!

The memory of the Porsche guy was still haunting me and I had learned that lesson. I asked for a vodka and diet coke "to calm my nerves" and that's when he said he knew I was special because I could be that honest about feeling nervous. I was just pleased he seemed quite normal, even if he did stare at my boobs a bit too much and had a silly floppy fringe. After a couple of hours, we agreed there was only so much diet coke you can drink on a date and in the car park we arranged to have another date the next weekend. Spoiler alert, I have now been married to this guy since 2005 – the floppy fringe went quite early on!!

His name was Mark and he was separated from his first wife. I liked him and despite my intention to play it cool and not jump straight in like I usually do, on the second date I had a glass of wine too many and told him my entire life story. I blurted it all out and I suppose it was a test to see if he ran. He didn't. That made me bolder. I waited until our fourth date to say "if you're just playing at this that's fine but please tell me. If you know this isn't going anywhere for you I'd like to know now." Get me. I found a voice to stand up for what I wanted. At last. It wasn't very subtle I know, it was very direct and in my heart it had a ring of neediness about it but he later told me it didn't come across like that. I didn't have lots more time to play with if I wanted children. Every time a relationship ended I realised more that I wanted children. We laugh now that I only wanted his sperm but joking apart I was looking for a potential father not just a boyfriend and I was on a mission. That said, he wasn't pushing the divorce process along and she refused to cooperate with him until he threatened to divorce her on the grounds of adultery. She didn't like that. In the end they waited for the 2 years' separation to kick in but in that time I realised he wasn't going to push things along with her to make it better with me. So on one hand I had clearly stated what I wanted but on the other I was putting up with him letting the divorce play out at his ex's behest. I wasn't sure how I felt about it but I let it play out.

During this time, he worked away during the week and only came back to Bristol at weekends. Long distance relationships are tough and I didn't want to be in one. During my second and third year at university my boyfriend (who I met when I was a first year and he was a third year) lived away and the pressure to make your time together be good is hard. It might be easier with mobile phones and other tech but it wasn't what I wanted. Mark is an engineer and he had a great job working at a Formula 1 team and I wasn't about to give him an ultimatum. I would never have the courage to do that as I wouldn't for one minute contemplate that someone would give something up for me.

His work had a summer party in 2003. It was a lavish affair with a seaside theme so there was a beach, playground for kids, candy floss stall, fairground rides and lots of other quirky stuff going on. It was an amazing party. I could see how much he enjoyed the trappings of that job and I asked him if he could ever see himself leaving. When he said no I got it but I told him that we didn't have a future. It wasn't an ultimatum at all, more a verbalising of my disappointment that he didn't seem to see the incompatibility of his job and a relationship with me. I meant it though as I wanted to move on if this relationship wasn't going to be the one that brought me kids. I think I had purposely kept something in me back to help me get through this disappointment that I probably felt was inevitable. The old thoughts kicked in, such as "things never worked out for me with men so why would this one be any different". I also think I was so damaged by my previous engagement ending and then the guy in between that I couldn't let myself believe in the relationship. To my utter surprise only a couple of days later he announced that he would leave his job and come back to Bristol. I couldn't believe it at first but he meant it and that is exactly what he did.

A few months later his house sold (the house he owned with his ex) and he moved in with me. By this time, I had moved into a rented flat down by the docks, in fact it was the flat that I missed out on that came back up for rental. Things have a way of working out sometimes don't they. I sort of wish I had let him find his feet after the house sale and moving back to Bristol, but I stepped straight in and made it easy for him and he moved in. I don't regret it but I do think I made it too easy. The reality was I was so grateful he had given his job up for me and moved back to Bristol that I thought I should help out. I knew it was a bit soon as we'd only been together 9 months, not that there is a "proper" time for these things, but probably too soon for me to trust that the relationship was going to last. Trust is such a massive thing for me and I don't trust easily, still don't, but I guess he had shown trust in me and our relationship to move back so I showed him some trust too. I've always thought it was just an easy path for him to take but my healing has allowed me to see another perspective - he was going through a divorce and it showed great trust to try again.

The next 12 months saw the end of the honeymoon period and reality kick in. The end of that fabulous early stage of staying up late talking, getting to know each other and lots of sex. I'm good at the getting to know stage but get so caught up in it that I lose myself so when it wears off I have no idea who I am in the relationship. We definitely had our ups and downs.

The first Christmas living together saw the turkey very nearly thrown in the bin. Turns out he's a bit of a grump at Christmas and I am so emotionally charged about Christmas, as you know, that it was pretty grim. There was another time we had a massive row and

I pulled all the CDs out of those tall Ikea CD racks and threw them on the floor. I was like a fishwife screaming at him. No idea why now. It was another moment of disassociation where I felt I was watching what was happening from the side of me. I now know that disassociation like that, to varying degrees, is no surprise for people like me who have suffered trauma.

On the whole though we rubbed along fine together and we bought the flat off the landlord and did it up. He's brilliant at DIY and we discovered I'm pretty good with a tile saw. I wish I had known how many tiles I would end up cutting over the years and I might not have been so good at it that first time! His divorce finally came through on Christmas Eve 2004, hallelujah! Two days later my Dad died. He was such a great support through all that.

On New Year's Day we went for a walk over the Clifton Suspension Bridge and into Ashton Court and there's nothing like a death to make you think about the future. I was prattling on about wanting children and understanding if he didn't want to get married again but they (they?!) would have to have my surname not his. Next thing he's got my hand and he's looking me in the face telling me he wants kids with me, but he wants to be married first. I stare at him not sure what he's saying and he asks me to marry him. He asks me to marry him. He took me completely by surprise with that proposal.

Like most things in my life I am so impatient I just can't wait and I had stolen his thunder a little bit by talking about having kids. He'd planned to ask me that day. I was taken aback, not expecting what I wanted to actually happen. I've just realised writing this that this was my first experience of manifestation. I had told him what I wanted and I got it. Many years later writing this, I see that I got exactly what I wanted but I've been so caught up in my past triggers and patterns that I can only see it now. Ok this is quite a moment ….

First though we have my Dad's funerals to get through and then we go straight into planning our wedding which is booked for 6 months later. We organise it all, we do it our way and we have a fabulous day with our families and friends at a hotel on the edge of the Mendips.

The one hiccup was my Mum, of course.

I was sort of in touch with my Mum, the occasional phone and even less occasional meeting up. I wasn't sure she would even want to come to the wedding, such was my feeling of being a disappointment to her, but when I asked, she said of course she wanted to come. We got married on a Friday, and she arrived on Wednesday. I spent the Wednesday and Thursday on pins keeping her happy and taking her for lunch. I even managed to crash the car into a post, I was so flustered. I dropped her at her hotel early Thursday evening after a few glasses of wine and breathed a sigh of relief.

Mark and I were having dinner with friends who were staying at the hotel we were getting married in and mid-way through the meal my Mum wandered in pretty drunk, making a scene. I was mortified. She'd got a lift there with another guest and they thought it would be fun to come and say hello. It was so awful. I can't remember how we got rid of her, but somehow we did.

I stayed in the hotel that night and the next morning, as I was getting ready, she appeared again, drunk, already making a spectacle of herself. Being rude to people, staggering around unsteady on her feet and asking why there was nothing to drink in my room. I am so used to her show that I just let it play out but I was so mad and upset that she couldn't just give me one day. Quite a few of my friends were keeping an eye on her during the day and eventually she did us all the favour of passing out. She was put to bed in a room and everyone let out a sigh of relief.

There had been a little bit of rain in the morning but by the time we got married at 11am the sun was out and it stayed out all day. I'd wanted to get married early so we had as long as possible to enjoy the day. We walked out of the ceremony to the theme from "The Muppets" which made everyone laugh. I've always loved the Muppets; I used to watch them every week with my younger brothers, but I've never quite known why I liked them so much. Recently I listened to a podcast where the guest said he was a Muppet fan and when asked why he replied that they know they are bad at what they do but they just get on with it anyway and love it. I think that's why I love them, because no matter what disaster happens or how bad it gets the show must go on. I am a Muppet!

It was a day of laughter and love and

naturally there was a Scottish man in a kilt showing us exactly what he wore underneath it. Our first dance was to *Be Mine* (written and performed by David Gray from the A *New Day at Midnight* album) because the song means so much to both of us. Here's a taster of just the first verse:

From the very first moment I saw you
That's when I knew
All the dreams I held in my heart
Had suddenly come true
Knock me over stone cold sober
Not a thing I could say or do

I thoroughly enjoyed my wedding day and it was so special having all our friends there with us to celebrate.

Mark and I had managed to get 3 weeks off work so we could do a few things we wanted to do for our honeymoon. It started with a Madness outdoor gig the day after the wedding which was a present from friends. I'm not that keen on Madness to be honest but it was good to have a plan for that day. We were shattered and the gig was quite rowdy so we hung around on the side, chilling in the sunshine. We were supposed to be staying in a B&B nearby that night but we decided to go home to our own bed instead. We had a couple of days at home and then a day at Thorpe Park amusement park as we both love amusement park rides, except I don't like the ones that spin you round. That was a great day out. Next we went to the Glastonbury music festival which was amazing. It was the second time we'd been and it was a year that lots of tents got washed away on the Thursday night as the rain was so bad. We thought we were unlucky having to camp near toilets (the smell?!) but it was at the top of a hill and we were dry so we were quite lucky really. We had an amazing time at Glastonbury, lapping up the curious sights, the music and the food. We managed to drink a lot of cider too.

During 2004 we had applied for visas to emigrate to Australia. We were told it would take ages. Mark made a comment one day about wanting to live in Australia as he had been there with his first wife and loved it. I had been twice by now (one of the London party girls moved to Sydney so I went to visit) and I said "Why not?" and it went from there. There were lots of hoops to go through but our visas didn't actually take ages and they came through just before our wedding. It was great news but it also meant we had to change our honeymoon plans. We'd wanted to have a relaxing time somewhere hot but instead, after Glastonbury, we flew off to Australia to validate our visas. We had to visit Australia within a year of the visas being granted and we then had five years to emigrate. We had 2 days in Singapore with very little sleep due to jet lag followed by 3 days in Perth and 3 days in Sydney so we could see the east and west coasts. It was exhausting and it wasn't the best way to investigate where we might emigrate to. It was done and visas validated, we flew to Nairobi for the main part of our honeymoon. Safari.

We had 1 night in a hotel in Nairobi. It was a stunning hotel with an amazing pool and a waterfall. It felt very safe too, with armed guards and a tall, imposing fence around the perimeter! I guess we were supposed to feel safe but I found it quite unnerving and even more so when we saw on the TV that bombs had gone off in London that day. We didn't live in London but being so far away from home I think we felt it more somehow and it was a rather subdued start to the trip.

The next day we were up early to join a 5-day safari trip with 3 other couples. It was the most amazing adventure. The animals were breathtaking and it was such a privilege to see them in the wild. The sunrise balloon ride over the Masai Mara was awesome and as I looked down to see giraffes running on the plains I remember thinking that life probably doesn't get any better than this. We saw lions, elephants, zebras, antelopes, cave buffalo, hippos and rhinos. Lots of my favourites, giraffes. It was like a dream. The 5 days whizzed by and then we flew back home and back to work. Back to earth with a bump but with wonderful memories to treasure.

By our first wedding anniversary I was pregnant, we moved from our third floor flat to a house across the road and in the autumn of 2006 our first son was born. It had been quite an easy pregnancy and the summer was so hot I was glad to be working long hours as the office was air conditioned. I'd wanted a home birth. My Mum had me in hospital but the 3 boys were all born at home (I think the next one after me might have been born in an ambulance but the 2 youngest were definitely born at home). I don't think it was a desire to emulate my Mum but her experience had taught me that a home birth was an option. However, I was 37, which was old for a first time mum (I was told), and the hospital thought the baby was going to be big so when he didn't arrive on my due date they wanted me to give birth in hospital. The labour was long and a bit hairy at the end but eventually he was born 7 days late after 33 hours in labour weighing 7lbs 8ozs. Not that big after all! Our second son followed 20 months later. I was not myself during my second pregnancy to the extent that I questioned if we should even have the baby as I didn't know how I'd cope. I felt wretched a lot of the time but after some investigations an iron deficiency was diagnosed as the problem and a course of iron tablets soon had me feeling better. My second delivery was the total opposite of my first; they didn't seem to care about my age or the size of the baby and I had a fabulous homebirth with just a midwife and my husband there and he was born after only 4 hours in labour weighing 9lbs. I had no interventions, no drugs and I said to myself "If I can do that I can do anything". I was on top of the bloody world. I was 39, 2 boys under 2 and I was knackered but I had my family.

We were tentatively thinking of emigrating to Australia around March 2007 but I got pregnant much quicker than expected and once we had a family my desire to emigrate waned significantly. I poured my energy into growing my longed for baby, working and being a mum. There wasn't much left over to plough into planning a move to the other side of the world. I told Mark that I would still happily go but he had to plan it. I knew that the chances of him doing that were slim but the original feeling of "why not" was still there so if he had planned it we would have gone I think. He didn't plan it and we didn't go and over the years we have talked about it and whilst we did want to go when we applied for visas we don't regret not going. "Home is where the heart is" and our hearts were here in the UK.

I went back to my law job for 3 days a week after 7 months' maternity leave with both boys. The second time was in February 2009

and the effects of the 2008 financial crisis were just taking hold. Property wasn't in a good place and I wasn't that keen on returning to my old job as a commercial property solicitor so I took advantage of the opportunity to look at vacancies in other parts of the firm that had been made available rather than making people redundant. I also fancied a change and hopefully something a bit less stressful.

I wasn't a partner but I had been a senior member of the property team and I moved to a team dealing with negligence cases against professionals. The clients were the insurance companies who insure companies, firms and individuals against professional negligence and if a negligence claim is made the claim is either dealt with directly by the insurance company in-house (particularly at the early stages) or they use what are called claims handlers to manage the claims for them. I moved to a team as a claims handler and they were interested in my property experience as a lot of property related claims came out of the 2008 financial crisis. I was still a solicitor but I was doing a job that didn't require me to be a solicitor so it was very much seen as a backwards move. I took a 35% pay cut but it was worth it for less stress.

I had to learn all the new jargon and how that team wanted the work done. I was being supervised by someone who used to be my peer and was now my superior. It was an interesting time. I relished the challenge of something new and there was a lot of work but I took to it well. Within 6 months I was promoted to supervisor and had a modest pay rise but nowhere near the cut I had taken. I was promoted because they had a new account coming in and needed someone to supervise it and the boss thought I would be that someone. We had a whole new team so I was leading a team of 4 plus me on a brand new account having been in the job 6 months. The volume of work that came in was beyond anything I had ever experienced and I was used to being extremely busy. I was drowning and agreed to do 4 days a week until we got on top of it.

We all worked hard but I took by far the brunt of it and worked regular 12 hour days with no breaks. I did the nursery drop off in the morning and Mark did the pick-up and bedtime so I could work late. This went on for 8 months during which I started to grind my teeth at night so badly my teeth hurt every morning. I was exhausted. I hadn't asked for help and no-one had seen fit to give me any.

I have always struggled with asking for help. In childhood there was no help to be had so what was the point of asking. It was a skill I never learned. To be honest I am still not very good at it now but I am trying. I recognise now when I need help even if it's after the event I can see that I needed help and could have asked for it. It's a step in the right direction and a step closer to asking for help in the moment.

Law firms are not big on pastoral care. I know that is a phrase more commonly used in education settings but it is based on traditional models of social and spiritual support found in all cultures. In a work situation it is looking out for people's general welfare in the work environment but not directly about their actual work. I am writing this in 2020/2021 when the UK, like most of the world, is largely working remotely as a result of the Covid-19 global pandemic. I have many friends working at home who have virtually no contact with their workplace and there is no-one looking out for their overall wellbeing. I am sure remote working is here to stay and some sort of pastoral care is essential in my view. I have heard of community managers who perform what sounds like this sort of role and I think the wellbeing of staff needs to be higher on the agenda for most companies.

Off my soapbox, now where was I? I am struggling. I finally decided we are on top of the work enough for me to go back to 3 days a week which I do for another 18 months or so. I like the job, the fast pace of the work and I like reviewing claims. I found I could quickly make a decision as to whether the claim had any substance. I liked leading the team but I was forced to do it in line with how my manager wanted it doing and it didn't work for me. I had no management training and it's hard managing people properly. I cared about them but I wanted the work done properly as well. There was a high turnover of staff which made it more difficult. I was devastated when I was taken aside one day and told one of my team had accused me of bullying them. I am a lot of things but I am not a bully so I knew something was not right. They didn't want me to speak to her but I did as I didn't want it left like that. I wanted to re-establish a connection with her and find out what was going wrong. It was a hard conversation to have, for both of us, but so worthwhile. I understood that the pressure I was getting handed down to me meant I wasn't acting like myself which is why it was going wrong. From then on I took less notice of the pressure from above and made sure I was acting with integrity as much as I possibly could. When I'd corrected the very same mistake in work for the fifth time in a week I found it hard to be patient and kind but I can hand on heart say I tried my best with what I had available to me at that time.

I was working 3 long days a week, always on catch up. Two small children to get to nursery in the morning on work days and on non-work days I had them all day. It was a tough time and if I could go back I certainly wouldn't do so much. I was good at my job and gave my all. 80% of my all would have been enough. I could have spoken up about the workload and said I was struggling. Pride got in my way and as a result I wore myself into the ground and I still grind my teeth 10 years later. It's a habit I can't seem to break. I have a mouth guard I wear at night to protect my teeth from breaking. Sexy. Not.

In 2011 I decided to leave my job. I had had enough and my boys were about to start school. They are only one school year apart and were due to start nursery and reception at the same time. There were a number of people in my team with school age kids and whilst I was happy working with the boys at nursery, the school day is shorter and I didn't want to have to work school holidays. I took the plunge and decided to leave. There was no plan other than settle the boys at school and see what happened.

We embarked on some work on our house which kept me busy and I also did an Indian Head Massage course as well as a Reiki 1 course. I enjoyed the courses and they were a start on a path of my interest in wellbeing. I haven't taken any of them any further but I learned valuable things from them. If I'm not sure what to do at any time I gather information and sometimes it's about gathering information on what is not right as much about what is right. Indian Head Massage is a fabulous treatment and I learned the real magic of touch. We practised on each other and then had to ask friends to be case studies. I loved my scalp being massaged as well as my arms and hands. How often do we have our hand held? Not that often. It is a powerful experience in the right environment.

The friends who were my Indian Head Massage case studies enjoyed the treatments but I knew I didn't want to do that as a job. I realised I like having treatments but don't get much out of giving them. I did learn some basic massage techniques which came in handy when I needed them with my son. You just never know when something will come in useful. As for the Reiki, I didn't follow on from the first course. What I got from that was entirely different. As part of the course we had 2 treatments from the Reiki master tutor. Reiki is a hands off treatment and performed fully clothed. It is energy work. My first treatment was calming and relaxing but nothing more than that. The next day my second treatment blew my mind. As she worked down one side of my body and then started moving up the other side, I could feel this sort of wave washing up my body that I just couldn't stop. The wave moved up my legs, my torso and before I knew what was happening I was sobbing uncontrollably for quite a few minutes. The sadness was overwhelming. She held me and once I'd calmed down she told me she had felt it the day before but also felt my resistance. By letting go that day I began to realise how much grief and sadness I had inside. It was a tiny step towards the awakening that was to come.

Out of the blue 6 months after leaving my job and just after signing up for the Indian Head Massage course, I was contacted by a man from the insurance company I used to do the claims handling for in the law firm and he asked if I would consider writing a monthly risk management paper for him to cover someone on maternity leave. I didn't know if I could do it but he persuaded me to give it a go and I agreed. It was perfect, apart from having to do the Indian Massage Course at the same time for 3 months. I worked from home and reported to only him which was amazing as it was such a big company. I thought about possible topics unless he had one he wanted me to do, we agreed on the topic and I researched and wrote it. It was 2,500 words each month and sometimes it was accepted on the first draft and sometimes I had to rewrite it a few times. It was interesting to do and I learned a lot about the insurance side of the claims and other areas of law. Some months it was tough to think of topics and those were hard to write. On the whole it went well and although it was only supposed to be for a year, it ended up being two and a half years. It only ended when the man I reported to retired. Whatever it was he saw in me that made him ask me to do it gave me an insight into risk and compliance and also writing. It was a pivotal point in my legal career and my life. Writing this now has made me realise he was another person who believed in me and my ability to do something. I still couldn't see this for myself.

About a year before the writing job ended I knew it was going to end and I contacted someone I used to work with who had started their own law firm. I told him what I had been doing since I left property, about the negligence claims handling experience and the risk management writing and I asked him to consider me for any non-solicitor jobs he might have as his firm grew. I didn't want to go back to being a solicitor but I wanted to use my experience in a different way if that was possible. I met him and his business partner for a coffee and a short time later they asked me to do some work auditing files. It was the odd day here and there but soon became 1 day a week which I managed alongside the risk management writing.

The firm was still small in those days and I got to know everyone over time. It was so different to being in a big firm where you didn't know everyone in your department let alone the firm. I got involved in a few different projects and turned my hand to all manner of things. It was flexible so I could manage the work around the boys and family life and they paid me for the work I did. Everyone was happy. It just grew from there. It became 2 days a week and then 3 once the risk management writing ended. The firm got bigger and bigger and it was great to have been there from early on so I knew the people and knew how things were done.

After about 2 years I became the Risk and Compliance Officer and was the go to for risk and compliance queries as well as property related ones. I wasn't asked if I wanted that role it was just given to me and like the people pleaser I am, I took it. If I had been asked I would have been flattered and would probably have taken it but I like to think I would have asked for clarification on what it actually entailed. Instead I just smiled compliantly and then worried endlessly about whether I was doing it right.

I reported to the two joint managing directors and was known for getting things done. I loved the interaction with the people; I loved helping them with their queries and pointing them in the direction the firm wanted them to go in when they weren't sure. It was a lot of work juggling people from many different offices and trying to bring them all into one way of working. I had several moments of tears; I wanted to help people as much and as quickly as I could and that isn't easy to sustain, especially as the firm quadrupled in size while I was there. I had a few conversations with my boss about it being too much and worrying that things were getting overlooked. I took it very seriously and took enormous pride in doing my absolute best. A lot of the time that was to the detriment of my family who got the exhausted, ratty and impatient me at home as all my energy was used up at work.

In 2016 it was time to get me some help. I was desperate for help but what had happened in the previous job, where I had been accused of being a bully, put me off managing people. I told myself I wasn't good at managing people so I shouldn't do it and I was better off working alone. Before I left the job in 2019 I had worked with 3 assistants and when the first 2 left they gave me lovely cards telling me how much they had enjoyed working with me and how much they had learned. I was truly touched, and a bit surprised. The first one I thought could be a fluke but when the second one said it too I thought maybe it was true. When I told the third one I was leaving she burst into tears; I hadn't expected that. We got on well and she had taught me such a valuable lesson (which she didn't know about at that stage) but I didn't realise I had had that much of an impact on her. It turns out I am good at managing people when I have the freedom to do it in my own way. Particularly when I get great people to work with too.

CHAPTER 19

At the age of 7, I was put on my first diet to get into the bridesmaid dress. That was the summer I was deemed to look acceptable, if you remember. My Mum watched what I ate all the time after that and I learned to eat in secret so she wouldn't know. Anytime I had some money I would sneak off and buy sweets and wolf them down before I got home. In my teens, after a big meal and I was complaining about feeling uncomfortably full, my Mum showed me how to be sick if I'd eaten too much, but I couldn't do it. I tried again many times as I realised it was a way to eat as much as I wanted but not get fat. I tried hard to make myself be sick but I couldn't make it happen. I was gutted then but I am so glad now.

In the days before the alcohol really took hold, my Mum used a lot of laxatives and I now think she was probably bulimic too. She had issues with her weight for as long as I remember which is why she did her best to stop me eating. I believe she was coming from a place of love, of not wanting me to be as unhappy with my body as she was with hers, but it just made me feel so much shame and I ate to fill the hole. What a mess. That was one generational pattern I didn't avoid.

The hole is deep and dark, like a well that you can't see to the bottom. It's not cold like that well, it's warm and pulsating. It's alive but not in a free and joyous way, more a desperate and sometimes fierce kind of alive that means it will do anything to get what it wants. It wants to be full, it wants to stop wanting more, it wants to stop needing. Yet it is never any of those things. There is always a need and a want for more. Whether it is a need or want doesn't matter, is never considered, the feeling of having more is all that is desired and it pulsates and writhes asking for more all the time until the mind gives in and helps the body find more for the hole.

Ahhhhh, the relief is almost instant. The first bit is in the hole and the writhing stops for a moment and the pulsating swallows up that bit, waiting for more. At this stage there will always be more, a lot more, the hole knows what is happening. This is what it wanted. It is getting what it wants. The pulsating and the writhing gradually slows with every new bit until finally there is no more and the hole knows that is it for now. There is stillness, momentarily, it looks like calm but it isn't.

It's the start of the next stage, which begins almost as soon as the last bit of more is in the hole. The banging, the clanging, the noise. It's so loud making the body shake. The hole is powerful, it controls the body and the body has to do as the hole wants. Yet the feeling in the hole is empty, even though it has what it wants. It is desolate, unable to feel or do anything now it is full yet it is still a hole. How can that be? The pulsating and writhing has stopped for now but it will be back again soon. It always comes back. In the meantime, the noise continues. It's not a happy sound, it's sad and mournful and loud and brash all at the same time. It is everything and yet nothing. Nothing and numb are the words that the hole would say if it could talk. Nothing followed by numb followed by nothing followed by numb. The cycle continues.

The hole inside me told me it was empty because I was worthless, I was useless, I wasn't loved. The only thing to do was feed it and at least then it was quiet for a little while. The only trouble with this is that more food equals getting bigger and as I used food to quieten the void I got bigger and bigger, became more of a problem to clothe and more visible. This in turn made the void bigger and it needed more food to quieten it.

The vicious cycle of eating to quieten the void went on and on and made me feel even more worthless, useless and unloved. In a society where thinness is celebrated and fatness scorned, as a fat girl I felt worthless. Every day I saw evidence in the mirror that I was obviously useless as I couldn't get the weight off. I didn't feel loved as I felt quite clearly that I was expected to lose weight. The voice inside me kept telling me to eat, that if I ate the sad feeling would go away. It did go away, for a short while, but it came back, every bloody time it came back. As I became more miserable, the more I ate and the bigger I became. For someone trying to play small it was, on the face of it, a strange strategy as the bigger I became the more noticeable I became. However, the bigger I became the real me inside had more to hide behind and my fatness became my armour that nothing could pierce.

It affected my early friendships as I always felt second rate. I wouldn't go shopping with them as there was never anything I could buy. Changing rooms were usually communal when I was young and the idea of getting changed in front of people filled me with dread. I just couldn't do it. Describing the inner void when you feel like this is difficult. If you know, you know. If you don't, all I can liken it to is that feeling when you're extremely hungry and your stomach feels like it's an empty hole and you just have to eat. I mean really have to eat. The thing for me though was I never got that hungry as I ate as often as I could because that feeling wasn't that I needed food but I needed love, warmth, kindness, acceptance. Food quietened the feeling for a short while but then the self-loathing, the utter disgust at what I had eaten would wash over me and the void would open up again.

Over the years, I have blamed my weight for many things. Failed relationships mainly. I have let it stop me from doing things if I was going to be embarrassed, particularly if I had to be weighed. Sometimes I have managed to overcome the potential embarrassment for something I have genuinely wanted to do. Like a zip wire ride in 2019 for my 50th, and when I was weighed I asked the lady to write it high on my hand so I cover it with my sleeve; she was very nice about it and discreet. For the rest of the day, I was super-conscious that my weight in kilograms was written on my hand and I couldn't wait to get back and scrub it off. I'm glad I did the zip wire, though. In the past I would not have done it because of my shame around my weight and my body.

For a long time, my weight provided me with an excuse for feeling unfilled. I could always blame my weight; in my head, I had this little voice that said my life was rubbish because I was fat. That gave me some comfort. Filled with the confidence of my home birth and the "if I can do that I can do anything" feeling, in 2009 I started Lighter Life which is a very low-calorie food replacement diet where you attend a session every week to be weighed and buy another week's "food". By food I mean packets of shakes and soups and bars. After the weigh-in, there was a group session where we talked a bit about feelings and other stuff, mainly food. For the first time ever, I sat in a room with other people who also talked about eating a whole packet of biscuits in minutes without tasting them or eating a whole baguette on the drive home from the supermarket. The group sessions weren't proper group therapy but I did get something from them. To realise it wasn't just me was a revelation and quite a comfort. In those sessions, I felt like I belonged.

I lost 5 stone overall in about 5 months. It was amazing. I had stuck to the diet pretty much the whole time; it had been tough but I felt fantastic. I had to buy a whole new wardrobe of size 12 clothes. I hadn't ever been a size 12 before. The black-outs, the dizzy spells, not sitting down with my family for a meal for all that time seemed worth it to look at what was deemed more acceptable. Then I noticed that doors were being opened for me more, I was let into queues of traffic more often, and I realised that people were treating me differently. This made me angry. I was the same person on the inside, yet it seemed I deserved better treatment because now I looked more acceptable somehow on the outside. Some people who knew me, but not very well, actually thought I was ill and didn't dare ask me if I was ok. Friends celebrated with me and told me I looked fantastic. It was an exciting and confusing time.

I kept the weight off for a year or so and then slowly it started creeping back on. It took 7 years in total, and I was back to where I started, but I had learned a valuable lesson. Yes, I was slimmer, yes I had had nice clothes (that were by then too small) and shopping for clothes had been a pleasure for a while, but inside, the essence of me was still miserable. I learned that changing the outside hadn't changed the inside and my worst fears had finally come true. I was thin, but I was miserable. I still felt worthless. If diets were meant to work, you'd only need one and you'd be done. There would be no need for a diet industry. There is a diet industry and it feeds on the misery of people like me. It sells me this dream that when I've lost 5 stone, everything will be perfect. That's bullshit. I'd dared to lose the weight; I'd bought into the dream of happy ever after, and it turned out to be a lie.

This time it was different. I realised it was

a lie, not because I was worthless but because it's an outright lie. Being slim, losing weight, wearing size 12 clothes did not make me happy because it takes more than that. For now, at last, the shame of being overweight, the shame that had stopped me doing things, the shame that had allowed myself to be trodden on, overlooked and treated badly, was starting to shift. Slowly but it was shifting.

Whilst I was having therapy we did some work around my body image. I realised how I often referred to my body as "it" and I didn't feel like me and my body were the same person. I know that sounds weird but I think this is another example of how I disassociated, this time from the shame of having a body that seemed to be so unacceptable. The comments I had at home, the pictures I saw in all the media and the inability to find a good range of well-fitting clothes all seemed to point to my body just not being good enough. My conditioning over the years made this a very easy place for me to go and stay there.

My therapist suggested I started mirror

work, looking at just my face for first 5 minutes a day and then slowly increasing the time. It took about 4 days for me to be able to look at myself without squirming and 2 weeks to be able to do it without crying. When I looked at myself in the mirror I would be drawn to look in my eyes and all I saw was deep pain and sadness. I kept going and it gradually got better, I could look at myself and see more than pain, I could see the years etched on my face, the memories and eventually I could smile at myself. As I came to learn more about myself, my desires and my needs and meet those needs, I began to appreciate myself more and the way my body looked began to matter much less. I began to realise that the size of my body is the least interesting thing about me and if my body bothers anyone they are not worth bothering about. I think this saying is golden:

The people that matter don't mind and the people that mind don't matter.

During the time I was on the counselling foundation course, we had a daily check in at the start of each day to say how we were feeling. I remember saying one day that I felt different. Where I usually felt that I had a thick line running right across my middle that cut me in two, like I somehow felt different above and below that line and there was a void in the middle, this particular day I felt that the sides had integrated and whilst there was still a void in the middle the sides were now connected to the top and the bottom. I didn't understand it but I knew that's how I felt. I was on the road to recovery and was starting to become whole, I just didn't know it then.

Later I read a lot about intuitive eating. I don't profess to be an expert and what I am about to say about my eating habits is my experience; it is not intended to promote any particular attitude towards food because I feel that journey is a very personal one for every individual and we have to find what suits us. To me, intuitive eating is about listening to my body and giving it what it needs. I clearly remember during both my pregnancies craving meat and so I ate more meat. It was probably something to do with needing more protein but I didn't question it, I just ate more meat. Pregnancy gave me an excuse to eat what I craved. However, when I wasn't pregnant if I got a craving for something particular I would ignore it. I would tell myself that I couldn't have it. It felt good denying myself something I wanted as though I was somehow a better person for having enough willpower to stop myself. I have yo-yo dieted all my life and denied myself what I wanted on so many more occasions than I have given myself what I wanted. Yet I was still fat. Books I read told me that by denying myself what I wanted meant I no longer trusted the signals my body gave me and I had a disordered relationship with food. It all made so much sense to me.

I had tried everything else so I decided to try a more intuitive approach. I listened to what my body wanted and how much. I ate a lot of ice cream the first couple of days but once my body understood it could have as much as it wanted, it didn't want it anymore. It was so interesting to see how my feelings around food changed as soon as I wasn't being restrictive. It has been a gradual change over the last 2 years but I can definitely say I have a much better relationship with food now. I don't feel the need to binge and that is firstly because the void no longer needs to be filled and also because I can have whatever I want when I want it so there is no need to eat as much of something I like when I get the chance as I can have it again the next day if I want. So I have a better relationship with my body and with food. The journey continues.

CHAPTER 20

I hadn't had much contact with my Mum for a few years before our wedding so it just went back to the way it had been. She made a bit of an effort every now and again and she came down to stay with me once when my first son was 2 months old. That was the only time she came to Bristol. One of her dogs was missing on the morning she came down so she spent most of the first day on the phone trying to work out if anyone had found him. Thankfully the dog turned up the next day. She drank quite a lot too during that visit but then again it was me who supplied it.

After that visit I didn't hear from her much and I only recall seeing her once at a family celebration. Out of the blue she started making much more of an effort and we spoke occasionally. I then discovered she was getting married again and she invited us to the wedding. The cynic in me thought she just wanted to put on a good show at her wedding with all her children there but the kinder me thought we should go and support her. I arranged a lunch a few weeks before the wedding so I could meet her husband-to-be and she could see my oldest son again (who was 8 by now) and meet my youngest son for the first time (he was 6). The lunch was strained but the boys were a great distraction and it went as well as could be expected I suppose.

I went to the registry office wedding with Mark and the boys. My brothers were there too. It was a relatively low-key affair and it was a real mix of emotions for me. I was on pins but I tried to stay calm for Mark and the boys. My Mum turned up obviously drunk but she was nervous and I could see how much she was shaking. I was pleased to see her looking happy but I was also sad to see how much worse she looked health wise since I'd seen her 8 years before. When they exchanged their vows and got to the part about "…. forsaking all others til death us do part" my oldest son whispered loudly "Isn't this her third wedding?". It was hilarious and those of us that heard it had a proper giggle. After what happened with my Dad and an acrimonious end to her marriage to my Step-Dad, it was nice to see her happy. The reception was a quiet affair in a local pub and we had to leave after a couple of hours to get back to Bristol for work and school the day after. I didn't know then but that was the last time I would see her outside a hospital.

Contact became very sporadic again after the wedding but my 2 youngest brothers had more contact and let me know how she was doing. 4 years later whilst I was on the counselling foundation course at BCPC (Bath Centre for Psychotherapy and Counselling) she went into hospital for a few days with jaundice which signalled liver failure. She was in and out of hospital again for the next few months and just days after her 70th birthday she died. I went to see her twice whilst she was in hospital. The first time I had to pluck up courage as the spectre of her from my childhood loomed large, particularly as I had been reliving a lot of it during therapy. I was very nervous but I knew I had to go. A friend suggested it might help if I could decide what I needed to get out of the visit and do it for me. That helped me summon up the courage to go and I decided that if she was awful to me that would be information to take into account when deciding whether to go again. I needn't have worried because after the 3-hour drive (my husband took me) what we found was a little old lady looking very frightened and not at all sure what to say. The spectre I had in my mind disappeared instantly. I found it hard to talk too so it was a lot of awkward silences and fake chuckles but we muddled our way through. Her husband was with her looking after her and it was nice to see her bossing him around, a little bit of normality. We stayed a few hours and then drove back to Bristol.

Recalling that hospital visit, I think I saw the real her that day. I suppose being very ill exposes the real person as there is no energy to keep up the facade. I can only remember seeing that once before on a day I was at her house watching the Wimbledon final for some reason (we were not big tennis fans). I was there on my own and I think it was the time I was living nearby so I was in my late 20s. She'd had a few drinks (you never knew how many) and she started telling me stories from her childhood. About how she hated being sent away to school and how she wanted her parents to love her. I saw her fragile inner child that day, just the once, and I got a glimpse of how unhappy she was under her steely exterior. Poor Mum.

The second time I saw her in hospital was a few weeks later and it was the last time. She was extremely ill by now and was barely conscious. I sat with her for a couple of hours while her husband nipped home. I held her hand and I told her that I loved her, even if we didn't always get on. I told her I was sorry that she was so ill but I hoped she wasn't in pain anymore. It was so sad but I had done a lot of grieving already for the relationship we never had so to say goodbye now was a bit easier. I drove away that day knowing I wouldn't see her again. She died 2 days later.

My oldest brother organised the funeral with her husband. It wasn't appropriate for me to get too involved so I didn't. The church was packed with old friends of hers and some of them I hadn't seen for many years. Lots of people told me how fabulous she was, what a ray of sunshine and how she was always so kind. I felt none of those things then and what I mainly felt was anger. I found it hard to contain my rage that day but I managed not to lose it. I was angry because she wasn't a ray of sunshine to me, she wasn't kind and I felt jealous that she was those things to other people whilst to me she was mainly horrid. I now see it differently but that is how I saw it then.

Back in Bristol, my friends told me how sorry they were for me and they didn't always understand when I said I was angry not sad. Grief is different for everyone and I read somewhere that it's complicated when you lose someone you are estranged from. When you lose someone you love and have a strong connection with, you are grieving for the loss of that person in your life. My Mum not being around anymore made precious little difference to my daily life and I felt confused by the grief. It was a lonely time.

I had now lost both my parents and I felt a bit cast adrift. Mark had lost both his parents too so at least we were cast adrift together.

I felt lucky to already be in therapy when this happened as I had a ready source of support. My Mum dying helped my therapy because there was nothing more she could do to me now. I had to process the past and how that affected my present and future but there would be no more opportunities for her to hurt me. There would also be no opportunity for reparation but I had long ago given up hope of that. I was pleased her last few years were happy and I was pleased she was no longer suffering. I was also relieved it was over but I was so sad for how awful it had been at times. Awful for me but also for her. I don't think she was happy a lot of the time, I mean really happy, content. I'm not sure she knew what that felt like. It is only now with the benefit of age and therapy that I can see how much she hurt and how hard she tried.

I look a lot like her and for years I hated that. I didn't like looking in the mirror and seeing her staring back. I have a lot of her in me and I have to thank her for that. I wish I was able to have more fun like she did and I suppose I could if I drank like she did but that is too high a price for me to pay. I was a challenge for her because I needed her and she didn't know how to deal with me. Neither of us are bad people, we were just a challenging match. Life with my Mum was never boring, bless her, and she was the only Mum I had.

Who are you?

*Standing proud, head held high, you are a
magnificent horse
At sunrise on a summer's day waiting to
gallop along the beach
Freedom!
You are rain
All who feel you cannot ignore you.
You weep like a willow
Cap pulled down low to hide your tears.
You are country music; an acquired taste!
You are diet coke straight out of the can
topped up with vodka to hide the truth; it is
9am.
You are a fish finger butty
quick and easy, no effort made at all.
You are a thistle, prickly and oh so sore.
You are bold, you are bright, you are my
Mum.*

CHAPTER 21

When it comes to our own private inner world we only have our version and have no idea what other people think or feel unless we can be courageous enough to share with others. We just don't know what is "normal" for others and until I went to therapy I had no idea that it wasn't usual to refer to your body as "it". I have always felt like my body let me down. With the benefit of hindsight, I can see that my outer body was the way I was demonstrating my inner turmoil; I'm not sure if I was hiding behind it, it was a buffer between me and the world or it was my way of showing up big when it all other respects I had to play small. I think the answer is it was a combination of the 3 and in my own way it was a cry for help.

I hated my body especially because it made me visible but for reasons I would rather not have been visible. Mind you looking back at photos I was never as big and grotesque as I imagined I was. "You've got such a lovely face". I used to hear that a lot and with it I also heard an implied "shame about the rest of you" every time.

About 18 months ago I was out walking in some woods with Bob the dog. It was at a time when my therapy was taking it out of me and I needed some time alone. It was a lovely cool but sunny day in spring, it hadn't rained for a while so underfoot was dry at last which was a pleasant relief from the ankle-deep mud of recent weeks and the dappled sunshine was pouring through the trees which were just beginning to get their coat of leaves for the year. It was perfect for a solo walk to rant silently to myself.

About half an hour into my walk I came across a tree that had fallen across the path. It was huge and there was no way over it. My options were to go back, go down the steep bank to my right or scrabble up the steep bank to my left. I wasn't going back so it was an up or down choice. I chose up. The bank was pretty steep so I walked back a little way to where the bank was a tiny bit less steep, gave myself a talking to and went for it. There were saplings and tree roots to help me pull myself up and as I took my first big step up onto the bank I realised that I was just standing there with my weight on one foot waiting to slip down again. I wasn't pushing on, I was just waiting to slide back down. That is how I had been living, a constant wait to slide back down from any progress I made. Something inside me said "Not any more" and I planted one foot in front of the other, big steps up the bank. I was hanging onto roots and small trees, making steady progress, and after just a few minutes I made it to the top. It felt amazing. I felt amazing. For the first time since my second son had been born I felt like I could do anything. I had the biggest smile on my face and I put my hands in the air and shouted "yes". I was so proud of myself but more than that I had showed myself I can do more than I think I can. It was a start of a new way of thinking.

As a result of that moment I came to understand that I didn't trust my body. I had spent so long hating it that I hadn't looked after it well at all and I didn't trust it. The words of an old colleague of mine came to mind when she said to me "I want to be strong again". I wanted to be strong. Well stronger. I wanted to be kind to my body and treat it better. I didn't hate it anymore. My therapy had made me see my body is me and by being kind to my body I am being kind to me and I deserve kindness. Also turning 50 I was aware of the aches and pains a bit more and I wanted to be able to move with more ease. My relationship with food had changed dramatically and now it was time to move.

I bought an exercise bike in January 2019. I'd had one years before and it had ended up being something to hang the washing on (don't they all at some time or another?) so I'd sold it. This new one folded up so it took up less space. I used it a bit but not as much as I thought I would. I'd left my job in June 2019 and when the kids went back to school in September I started using my exercise bike 2 or 3 times a week and going to aqua aerobics with a neighbour once a week. It felt good to be moving. I was listening to my body that was telling me it wanted to move more after all those years of being stuck at a desk. I also went back to swimming at the local pool; I find swimming lengths incredibly boring but I know it's good for me so I made myself go. I was getting into a good routine when we went into lockdown at the end of March 2020 due to the Covid-19 pandemic.

The pools closing was a real blow but I kept up the bike and did it every day Monday to Friday and walked with the dog at weekends. I was feeling brilliant by the end of lockdown in July 2020.

The other thing I wanted to do was get into yoga but I never quite managed that in lockdown either. However, as we came out of a lockdown a friend of mine told me she'd got into doing a short yoga session online every day and I decided to give it a go. I loved it. I have done yoga classes in the past but I was usually the oldest in the room, and the fattest, and I usually ended up hurting myself. I tried too hard to prove I wasn't as bad as they all expected I think. It was the right thing at the right time and I am still doing it nearly every day as I write this. It has been fabulous to see how slowly but surely I have become more flexible, stronger and the best bit is I believe in myself now. If I can't manage a pose I don't beat myself up, I just do what I can and know that the next time I do it, I'll be able to do a little bit more and so on. The breath work in yoga has transformed my breathing which in turn has given me an ability to calm myself down if I'm feeling stressed; I breathe in deeply putting one hand on my heart and the other on my abdomen, I breathe deeply into my abdomen so it moves outwards and as I breathe gently out my abdomen returns in and I say to myself "you are safe, I've got you".

10 years ago I ran the Bristol 10km with my friend. We'd been able to run 5km quite comfortably (it never got easy but we could do it) and we'd trained to get up to 10km. I've not run much since then and whilst I've had little forays into getting back into it, it has never lasted. I don't like running but I do like the way it makes me feel afterwards. Those endorphins are marvellous. I had been wanting to get back into running but I had a problem with my Achilles for about a year and then I had plantar fasciitis for just as long again. I'd given up hope of ever getting back to it and told myself I was too old. The yoga was helping me feel stronger and I thought my core might be better and I decided to give the Couch to 5k coaching app another try. I had done it twice before over the years but never got past week 4. I'd even done all the weeks twice to build up slowly but I always ended up getting injured. This time was much better. The work on the bike and the yoga had helped I think as I pretty much sailed through

weeks 1 to 4 with no problems. Then came week 5 and I'd obviously never got that far before because I was shocked by the way the running ramped up. I walked round the corner of my house one day as I was logging onto the app and was so shocked that I was supposed to run non-stop for 18 minutes that I said "what the fuck" out loud much to the amusement of my neighbour. I did it but as the runs got longer I had more rest days in between runs. I managed not to trash talk myself because I couldn't just go out and do it. I was kind and patient. In week 8 I managed to pull a muscle behind my knee and ended up having 10 days off running. In time I got back out and finished the 9-week plan which had taken me about 13 weeks in total and I was so pleased with myself, for myself. After 3 attempts, to actually finish it and run for a full 30 minutes was a good day for me. I want to keep it up but more importantly I have learned:

- To be kind to myself
- To be patient with myself
- To believe in myself
- To trust my body can do it
- That I am more capable than I imagined
- That it doesn't matter what I look like

- That if anyone laughs at me (which they do) they don't matter
- What matters is that I'm out there doing it
- That I am resilient
- That I am not too old
- That I am not too fat
- That I am only just beginning!

CHAPTER 22

It was during my time at BCPC in Bath doing the counselling foundation course that I came across the concept of "I". I was a late starter to this too but growing up my needs or wants weren't something I ever thought about; I was surviving. Later when I left home I stayed stuck in survival mode. I hadn't done much self-development or growth work by then and had only just started therapy so it was all new to me. I felt ashamed that I didn't know who "I" was. There was an exercise one day on the course where we sat on the floor and in turn we stood up and told the group how we thought we were different to everyone else. I stood up and said I was different as I had no idea who I was. One of the responses I got was that it must be scary being on the course every week having no idea who I was. Too right it was. To be acknowledged like that was a real gift; to be seen and heard. It was a step towards discovering my "I".

The real pivotal moment came when I went to a one-day workshop for IOPT - Identity Oriented Psychotrauma Therapy - in 2018.

This is a simple explanation of what I experienced - we worked in a group (maximum of eight) and each person took their turn to do a piece of work. The person doing the work put what they wanted to work on in a sentence of no more than seven words or characters and wrote it on a board. They then gave each member of the group one of the words to feel into. It's hard to explain but if I closed my eyes and just tried to feel the word in my body, rather than think about it in my mind, I found that I had an instinctive way of just knowing how to act and what to say about how I was feeling. Every time it made sense to the person doing the work even if it didn't always make sense to me. I'm sure it sounds very woo but it totally blew my mind.

When I was part of the group feeling into someone else's word I truly felt it and could express how I felt. When it came to my turn I asked "What don't I want to see?". There were only seven in the group so I had one word left over. Without thinking I gave every word out but "I". Some people could feel into their words but others struggled and the general consensus was that there was a feeling of nothing. Nothing. The facilitator was gently leading me around from word to word. She was a small, gentle and kind woman and I was gripping her hand tighter and tighter. When we got to "I" she gently and kindly told me that what was going on was I had no "I". God that was so hard to hear, see it embodied in the others and to feel it. It was like I didn't exist although I was there so I did exist. It was a big turning point for me and that led me to discover my "I" and I am pleased to say we are now well acquainted.

It took a lot of soul-searching and contemplation to get to that point but it was worth it. I did it mainly with the help of my therapist but also the work I had done up to then allowed me to accept the position much more easily than if it had happened pre therapy. I could see that I needed my "I" to feel whole. I wanted to be whole. Children of alcoholics in a codependent relationship with their alcoholic parent are highly susceptible to not having an "I". Their very being is subsumed by the parent; the parent's up is the child's up, the parent's down is the child's down. It is all consuming and the concept of self and the child's own wants and needs never matter. If you learn at an early age that no-one is interested in you, you learn to keep quiet.

Quite early in my time at therapy, I had a weekend away with 2 very old friends, an annual event. When I start something new I tend to throw myself into it and I spent a lot of the weekend talking about what I was learning in therapy. One of my friends told me that there were times when we were younger that she knew our friendship meant much more to me than it meant to her. Oof! That hit me hard, it took my breath away. It still does when I think about it. I admire her honesty and, whilst it was very hard to hear at the time and it has vividly stuck with me, I think it actually helped me in a roundabout way work out that I needed to find what I now know as my "I" and also to stop looking to others for validation.

I turned into a "good girl", another pattern that stayed with me for a very long time. It's the "good girl" and the having no "I" that ironically made me such a good worker – I would give, give, give. It was having no "I" that also meant I was so easily subsumed by my romantic relationships. That pattern, and the attendant need to play small, had been with me a long, long time by now. Finding our "I" is so important if we don't find it when we are younger but when we only know our own reality we have no idea that other people have a sense of self that just doesn't figure for us. I am so pleased I have found mine.

Once I'd found my "I", I must have stepped straight into it as it was less than 12 months later that I had a conversation with someone at work that changed everything for me. I was out at a meeting in early 2019 and a colleague, my then assistant, asked me cautiously if they could ask me a question. I'm pretty much an open book and I said "Yes of course". The question I got was quite a surprise, it was "Why are you the only one who is real here?". When I reflected afterwards I secretly hugged myself for now owning my "I" so well. I have found that happens a lot. As I own who I am, what I stand for, what I want, occurrences seem to happen out of the blue in line with those things.

Here I am after discovering and owning my "I" not only being told I am real but also it appears I am the only one being real. We had a long conversation about what that meant and what I stood for and why I was real and how it might be that others don't show up in quite the same way. It was unlike any conversation I'd ever had before – lawyers don't have conversations like that in my experience. I'd needed the armour I had hidden behind before as a crutch to prop me up and get me through life. Perhaps not to the same degree but maybe other lawyers hide behind an armour or a mask of sorts. The person who said this to me had only known me for a short while so hadn't know me pre-breakdown. Once the armour started to come off though there was no stopping it and there was definitely no putting it back on.

What also happened is that I started to question what I was doing at that job. At this time, I was listening to lots of podcasts about workplace culture and organisation and it gave me the language to explain what I was feeling. Put simply, my personal values were at odds with my experience at work and it didn't feel right. I had changed a lot in the last

2 years and the company had too as it started to get bigger and bigger. Previously, I had really only had one aim in life and that was survival. I wouldn't have even known about values. Now I'd had my eyes opened and my values were trust, support and integrity. I had a meeting with one of the bosses which did nothing to alleviate my concerns about the direction of the firm and I ended up leaving. I actually said I didn't want to continue with my existing role as by this time I was more interested in the people's experience of work rather than the work itself. Instead I wanted more of a people-based role where I could help people feel safe to be themselves at work and supported to do their job thereby improving their experience of work. It seemed so obvious to me that was needed and in fact I was already doing it alongside my risk and compliance job.

To my surprise they didn't see that what I was talking about was needed or wanted and as I was self-employed and no longer wanted the risk and compliance job, there was no job for me. Even though I had no formal notice period, I agreed to work for another three and a half months and I even found them my replacement. I hoped they'd find a role for me but they didn't and I was gutted they let me leave so easily as I had worked so hard to help them build the company. It felt like I was being abandoned all over again, this time by them letting me just walk away. I didn't even get a leaving present!

I was badly affected and I fell into a depression again. Not as bad as my breakdown but pretty bad. It was my choice to leave, I know, and I think I covered it up so well they didn't even know. It was with a very heavy heart that I left that job but it has turned out to be a blessing in disguise. I have since been able to spend time with my family during lockdown and not have to worry about work, worry about the money, yes (as I wasn't making any), but it was liberating to not feel beholden to a job as well as juggle the family. I have started my own business as a coach, I have started a podcast, I have written this book. If I hadn't had this time I don't know that I would have done those things.

My assistant and I are now great friends despite me being twice her age. We have long chats putting the world to rights and we meet on a soul level. She is an amazing lady and I will be forever grateful to her for opening my eyes to what could be possible for me.

Meeting of Minds

*You are a cheese plant with dark glossy
leaves
The always interesting delicious monster
You are an oak milk mocha at 11am on a
sunny and crisp autumn morning
Or a fun and fruity cocktail to start the
evening in a playful way
You are soul music, a warm heart beating
A cool forest, majestic in your serenity
With its blossom and berries, you are
hawthorn
giving food and shelter to many and more
You shine bright like a clever fox in the dark
without cunning, but knowing how to make
real what is in your heart
You are my fabulous friend with tiny hands
Who makes me think and care and laugh out
loud.*

CHAPTER 23

I have been lucky not to have had any major operations or ailments over the years. I've had the odd injection, blood taken and uncomfortable procedures and my way of getting through them is to close my eyes until it's over. It has served me pretty well in the past. That is until I find myself sitting in a big chair in Bristol Eye Hospital, my face is covered with a green cloth that exposes my right eye (the green cloth is the sort you see in operating theatres to cover everything except the surgery site), my eye is clamped open with a primitive looking device that looks more like an instrument of torture (am I being a tad dramatic?!) and a nurse is hovering over me about to put a large needle in my eye. I am shaking from the adrenaline running through my body and I am gripping the hand of another nurse very hard. I think she's regretting offering to hold my hand now. I am looking at the needle looming towards me and I know it has to be done but I don't like it one bit.

My eye has been cleaned and numbed and I don't feel the needle go in but as the liquid is squeezed into my eye I feel a rush of pressure and a weird sensation as it flows around my eye. The liquid is a weak solution of a cancer drug and the idea is it will cause the new blood vessel that is growing into the back of my eye to shrink away and the excess fluid that has caused my sight loss should drain away. It is unlikely to restore all my sight but it should improve things. Mercifully it is over very quickly. When the injection is done I get out of the chair and take a few seconds to steady my wobbly legs. Then, feeling like a baby deer learning to walk, I toddle off to find Mark who is waiting for me.

It has only been 4 weeks since I was in A&E at the eye hospital and today I have seen a consultant and he has brought me straight down for this treatment. In 10 to 14 days I should hopefully start to see some improvement. Eyes are amazing things and we so take them for granted. I'd had a huge panic when I thought I might go blind in this one eye and then possibly the other. I am extremely short-sighted and there has always been the risk of things happening but for this, which is unusual, to actually be happening has thrown me. For the first 2 weeks I couldn't judge depth as there was so much less sight in the right eye and I kept falling up and down stairs and falling off pavements waiting to cross the road. I must have looked drunk stumbling around. Oh the irony! Slowly though my eyes started to adapt and by the time I'm in the hospital having the injection, my left eye has taken over as the dominant eye and I am doing much better. My brain is compensating with the change in what I see and enabling me to carry on. Amazing.

10 days later and I can see a little bit better in my right eye. The patch of grey that I can't see through has shrunk a bit and it is not quite so dark grey but it is still there. I am supposed to be having 3 injections 4 weeks apart but when I go for the second injection I don't see the consultant and they tell me that there is no more fluid in my eye so there is no point having another injection. I realise at this point that my sight may not come back. It has been such a rollercoaster from being in A&E when the registrar told me the damage was permanent, then talking to my optician who was obviously angry that I had been told that but he was careful not to say the registrar was wrong and then seeing the consultant who

gave me hope that the injections may help. It seemed like this was as good as it was going to get.

Throughout this time, I had continued going to work but the strain to see the screen had led me to have a trapped nerve on one side of my neck and on the other side I had acquired what seemed to be a frozen shoulder. I was not a happy bunny. Like a lot of people, I carry stress and tension in my shoulders and upper back so I am used to aches and pains. I let it carry on for a few more weeks hoping it would go away and by the time I decided I had to get help I couldn't get a physio appointment for a week and all the doctor offered me was a nerve blocker that made me feel like a zombie. I took one and gave up on the pills. I finally got to see the physio and thankfully it helped. Just as well as we spent that Easter in a caravan and I was dreading it with my neck being so bad.

When I went back to see the consultant in late March I had still only had one injection and he wasn't happy with my progress. He thought it could be improved so I then had 3 more injections a month apart and by late June that year I had gained most of my sight back. I still had a small patch of grey but it was miniscule compared to what it started out like. The relief was immense. I could no longer wear contact lenses, sadly, and my cataracts are coming on nicely but I can see again and I treated myself to a funky pair of hexagonal glasses. They cost a small fortune because my prescription is complex but it was such a joy to be getting new glasses now my eye had stabilised.

It had been a tough time and I had largely hidden how terrified I was from my friends and family. I didn't want to be a nuisance and I thought I should be strong for everyone else. It was the old pattern of keeping my feelings in and not showing how vulnerable I felt. Partly because being vulnerable as a child exposed me to criticism and ridicule and partly because I'd had to take care of myself. As my eye stabilised and allowed the relief in, I began to unravel.

I was in weekly therapy with my counsellor for 3 years. It took me around a year to trust the process and understand that to move forwards I had to learn about myself. Finding the books of Brené Brown helped me understand shame and its antidote, empathy. The books also helped me embrace vulnerability. All these things are still a work in progress but what I have learned so far has changed me. I now understand myself so much more, how the past informs the person I am today and I am able to move forward taking those parts of me that I want to keep with me whilst acknowledging the other parts have helped me get to where I am now but are no longer needed. I am safe now and I no longer need to survive.

Earlier I mentioned that one of the tutors at BCPC would play a big part in my healing journey. In my first tutorial with her I told her how hard I was finding the course, how my feelings were all over the place and I was struggling. She suggested that I tell the whole group that at the open session at the end of the day. My mind was shrieking "No way" but my gut told me to do it so later that day I summoned up all my courage and told the group how I was feeling. It was my first experience of being truly vulnerable. It was hard but as I started talking it got a bit easier and when I'd finished it opened up a whole conversation in the group about how most people were struggling to some degree or other. Someone even thanked me for bringing it up. I was bemused by the whole thing, but the overwhelming feeling I was left with was relief; relief at having spoken my truth and relief that it had been accepted in such a positive way. It spurred me on to embrace vulnerability with both arms.

I believe that I lost the sight in my eye because I unconsciously yet steadfastly refused to see any of the signs that I had received earlier in my life pointing me towards the healing I needed to do. The relationships that had come my way, particularly the two with alcoholic men, and the minor ailments in my later years that were designed to slow me down. I was so set in my belief that I was fundamentally flawed and unworthy that I saw it all as my fault somehow, what I was due. I only deserved relationships that consumed me and where I had to be useful to be able to stay. That was my pattern. My relationship with my husband is a much healthier relationship. My realisation that time was running out to have children made me behave very differently when I met him. I didn't connect with him initially, I stayed distant to make the split easier if (when) it came and I laid my cards on the table very soon in our relationship; I wanted a commitment, I wanted children and I wasn't going to wait very long. It's funny now thinking about that as I had been so compliant in my previous relationships, so grateful for any morsel of affection. I had given up all hope of a fairytale, that story we are told over and over again as little girls. That story that in my lonely upbringing I hoped was true. That one day I would be rescued by a knight in shining armour and we would live happily ever after. So it was with very little hope of having a happy ever after that I embarked on my quest to have children.

I know this sounds very cold and calculating and it is not easy for me to write these things about myself. I was calculating yes but I wasn't cold. I was frozen from my experiences and I was terrified it was going to stop me having my own family that I desired so much. My husband, as he was to become, was separated from his first wife and reeling from her infidelity and the failure of his marriage. We suited each other right there, then. We didn't challenge each other on an emotional level, superficially we were what each other wanted. I was clever and attractive

with big boobs and he was handsome, steady
and stable and he made me laugh. I'm sure
relationships have been built on less but it
was not a fairytale. Or not a fairytale of my
child-like dreams. Maybe he was my knight in
a maroon coloured diesel Rover (nicknamed
the Beast by me). My very own modern day
knight.

Not that long ago a friend said that the best
thing that ever happened to me was meeting
my husband. I didn't like that one bit at the
time. I'm not sure why but possibly because I
wanted the best thing that happened to me to
be something I did. I have relied on myself
and only me for so long that I felt it was
befitting that the best thing had to come from
me. Maybe it did come from me, after all I
joined the dating website that we met on at
just the right time to meet him, but I think it
was more about fundamental things that I feel
a desperate need to control. Like trust. I don't
trust anyone really, never have. Not a
surprise with my history and still after years
of marriage I find it hard to trust him. It is my
thing not his. It is not that he is
untrustworthy, it is that I can't trust and to
say that he is the best thing that has ever
happened to me surely means I have to trust

in him, trust myself with him, trust that we are going to last.

We might not last but not trusting is just going to make it a self-fulfilling prophecy because if I don't trust it won't last. Of that I am sure. We have got this far. I trusted enough to get married, then to buy a house then to have kids but if I am honest I have always had one eye on how I'm going to cope when it ends. I have not fully given myself to what our relationship could be. As the kids get older and will lead their own lives we are getting to a stage of looking at our relationship anew. Will we last past them leaving school? Will we decide to call it a day and go our own ways? I have a strong feeling we will last. We still make each other laugh and we still know why we got together in the first place. I love him. It is a deep appreciation kind of love. It is not the "can't live without" kind of love that I dreamed of after watching untold films and reading countless books. I think I had that fleetingly with the man I was with before my husband and it broke my heart when that relationship ended. It was the worst thing and the best thing. I don't mind that I don't have that with my husband because it destroyed me when it was taken away. Not actually destroyed me but it destroyed a part of me, the part that trusted.

I am learning with my husband to trust in something else. To trust in him and to trust me with him. I am the one that I don't trust, not him. Ironically though he trusts me and I'm still learning to do that. I listened to a podcast not very long ago and the woman was talking about the very successful business she had built when her marriage ended. She was devastated and vowed to never need anyone again. She talked about building a protective shell around her so she couldn't be hurt again. I listened to that with such interest as I am trying to crack open my protective shell and let people in. My shell had been with me, protected me, kept me safe for over 40 years when I lost the sight in my eye and I started my healing journey but I want something more now. I want to trust, I want to experience what that feels like and at the same time I'm trying not to make it some fairytale thing that I chase and get disappointed by. It's a fine line for me, this trust thing, protection on one side and goodness knows what on the other side but I am curious now to take a step over and have a peak. There is trust right there in just that tiny step.

This is what I've got from losing the sight in my eye. The therapy journey, the healing and the new found appreciation I have for myself and my life. I honestly thought I had lost part of the sight in my right eye forever. If I looked at my children straight on I could no longer see their faces. What had happened was a curious thing and was due to me being so very short-sighted. If it happened to my right eye it could happen to my left and then I would be screwed. Yes, I was catastrophising a bit but there was, and still is, a real possibility that I will have such problems with my eyes that I will lose a lot of the sight, possibly go blind. It was only the other day that I was writing about this and I realised how bloody scared I was and how it feels like I have a second chance. It was a wake-up call in more ways than I realised until now.

This is my chance to lead a life that I want, a fulfilling life, not be scared. To make a difference, help other people, see my kids grow into adults and hopefully a lot more after that. If I can do what I can now, if the worst happens and I do lose my sight I will do so knowing I gave it a good crack. I had been waiting, like an aeroplane waits in a holding pattern for a landing slot, to come in to land. Writing this book feels like my landing. I don't have all the answers, far from it. I don't even have some of the answers but I do know I am different, that I am changed by my journey.

The other main player in my life so far has been control. I don't have many happy memories before about age 10 which worries me sometimes. It can't be that there is nothing to remember so for some reason I have blocked the memories from those years out. I suspect that it's a result of my Dad leaving and life changing so dramatically that it was as though that early part didn't exist. I did such a great job at playing the dutiful daughter and "good girl" when my Mum remarried that it was the easiest thing to pretend it never happened. It did happen, I have a few photos from that time and I have a few memories but they are scarce. It's a trauma response; I suffered trauma when my Dad left and my whole world was turned upside down. My Mum was upset all the time, she was desperate for the relationship with my Step-Dad-to-be to work, my brother and I were getting in the way of that and I felt the only thing I could do was be as good as possible. I grew up very quickly and soon learned that no matter how hard I tried I couldn't make my Mum happy. I tried so so hard.

For years I hoped my Dad would come back and take us away with him, I also hoped my Mum would someday just be happy and we'd all live …. can you guess …. yes happily ever after. Not knowing what had happened, where he'd gone, where he was, whether he was ever coming back, whether he was even alive, was unbearable. I used to think I became sad easily and I was a bit of a wuss but as I have walked my healing journey I have come to realise I am extremely sensitive, an empath. I feel other people's pain, I feel trauma deeply. I am on constant alert unless I make a concerted effort to shut off.

From the early years which I believe to have been happy, it all changed and carried on changing. First my Mum's wedding to my Step-Dad, then the change of my surname, new house, new school, new brother, another new school, expelled, another new brother, another new school, exams, more exams, leave for university. There were a lot of new things to deal with. Coming home from school I'd never know what I was coming home to, what mood she'd be in, whether I'd be able to get on with my homework or would I have to look after my brothers, do the tea and then get to do it about 8pm. Those were my favourite times when I could go to my bedroom in the evening and know I would be left alone. I watched TV for hours and did my homework. All I could control was doing my school work the best I could and I tried so hard.

I tried to control as much as I could so that my Mum wouldn't get mad; she was proper scary when she was mad and I tried as hard as I could to stop that happening. I'd do as many chores around the house as I could, I'd preempt what needed doing just to smooth things along. If I could control the environment maybe she'd be nice to us. That's where my desire for control comes from. When you grow up in chaos what you want most is order and control so when you leave home you do your utmost to control anything you can. I lived with others because I couldn't afford to live on my own in London but as soon as I could afford it I moved out as I needed to control who was in my space and when. I didn't really drink until I was 25 because of the need to be in control. The flip side to this though is that I have given away control in nearly every relationship I have had as I wanted love more than anything else. I have surrendered my control countless times which is why it hurt so much when those relationships ended. I think that's why I surrendered less control to my now husband as I somehow subconsciously knew I had to look out for myself in a way I had failed to do before.

Trust and control are themes that have weaved throughout my life and I'm still not entirely sure of their relationship to each other and their relationship to me. My husband used to call me a control freak when we rowed in the early days and I can see what he meant but I didn't know myself that I had to be in control just to survive or that's how I had felt growing up. I wish I'd been more of a rebel but it wasn't safe and if I had I wouldn't be the me I know today and I like the today me. I wish I hadn't had to go through all I went through, I wish it hadn't affected me as much as it did. However, those things have made me who I am. My innate ability to have empathy for others and my desire to help others are things I love about myself now.

I am quite a spiritual person these days and I often pull an oracle card or two. Recently the cards I pull have been telling me that the suffering is over and its time to shine. That it's time to share myself with the world. It sounds like it really is time to land.

Found

The light is so bright, I can hardly bear it.
Too many years in the dark
I've always been there, hoping and wanting
but it looked like she was never going to
hear my cries.
Yearning for a place in her world,
to feel loved and cherished was all I ever
wanted
but conditioning had taught her otherwise.
To be needed and useful and pleasing
was how she found her way.
She lost me in the process.
but it was that "process", that bloomin
process
that brought us back together.
I am found, I am home, I am loved and
cherished,
I am seen, I am heard.
This is me!

CHAPTER 24

Here it is, the ending of this book. Now I don't know about you but when I watch a film or read a book I feel cheated if there isn't a happy ending. I always want the happy ending and given the number of references in this book to me wanting a fairytale ending, wanting someone to come and save me, I am guessing you're not surprised by that.

I have one last story to share with you. At the end of the year at BCPC (July 2018) we all had to do a 20-minute review. There was no formal structure to the review and we could do what we wanted. Some people showed a video, some sat us in a circle, some sat in their usual chair. In my last tutorial, I had talked at length with my tutor about the year and I had come to the realisation that being on that course was not about being a counsellor, not for me. Each day on the course had propelled along my therapy and personal development and I had learned so much about myself. She helped me see what it had been about. Preparing for my review, I wrote out pages and pages of notes and I practiced out loud in the car as I was driving. Every time I said it out loud it changed and I was starting to think I wouldn't be able to do it. I had bought a new outfit - bright green jeans, a bright pink vest top and a blue linen shirt. Subtle; not! On the day in question, wearing my bright outfit, I was nervous but I did the one thing I always knew I was going to do and I stood up at the front of the room to speak to the group. I paced slowly up and down as I told them my story of being on the course. I didn't have notes as I wanted to say what came from my heart that day. I told them snippets of my story to give them an idea of how I came to be on the course. I told them how every day on the course had been such a challenge but also a privilege and how happy I was to have that experience with such a great bunch of people. I thanked my tutor for her encouragement and her ability to see what I needed and guide me to see it too. I then told everyone how the course had not been about becoming a counsellor for me, it had been about that very moment there, standing in front of them wearing my new outfit and being able to say to them "This is me" and believing in my heart that this me is enough. As I said those words I looked around the room and saw the teary eyes of my tutor and the beaming faces of the group willing me on. It was a magical moment that even today, writing about it, conjures up so much emotion for me. It was my "I See, Me" moment.

So I am pleased to say there is a happy ending but not quite the one I hoped for when I was younger. No knight in shining armour on a trusty steed. I got my happy ending but not because someone came and saved me. I got my happy ending. Me. It took a lot of work to get here and it will always be a work in progress but as I type this I can say categorically that I am the happiest I have ever been. It has been hard work at times, therapy wasn't easy, there have been tantrums, weekends in bed, many rows with Mark and the boys, I quit my job and started a totally new business. It has been a rollercoaster for sure but now I am here, particularly out the other side of my therapy, I wouldn't change a thing. I honestly wouldn't. My life so far has made me who I am, a gloriously incomplete human being who is glad to be alive, who is thriving, who is living a life that makes her heart and soul sing. It may not be this way forever, there are bound to be more hard times, but for now I am riding the crest of this wave and if it crashes I will regroup and see what happens next. I am equipped with the knowledge of how good it feels to be me in my life right now today. I know I can do it and I can do it again after the next storm passes.

We have challenges to come in our family but we will face them together with the best we can bring at the time. I hope my business will grow so I can help people feel less alone and discover their gifts. I will begin volunteering for Nacoa very soon, the National Association for Children of Alcoholics, as it is important to me to give back. Nacoa provides amazing support to children of alcoholics (whatever their age) and I just wish they had been around when I needed some support. I applaud the work their amazing ambassadors do to spread the word about their work. I also applaud the fabulous campaigners out there trying to raise awareness about the damage caused by the stigma surrounding alcoholism which prevents people who need help from seeking it. Drinking culture is inherent in our society today, it is expected and celebrated, but as soon as someone has a problem with their drinking they are shunned. The shame surrounding alcoholism is astounding. This has to change for the sake of all the people affected by alcoholism, not just the alcoholic themselves.

There still seems to be this belief that it's only the alcoholic that needs help but the disease affects whole families. There also appears to be the belief that if you are removed from the situation causing the harm then everything is suddenly all right. It makes me very angry thinking about that. The damage caused by the trauma is with us forever and unless we find ways to come to terms with it, it will eat us from inside and given the chance it will repeat itself with the next generation. If this applies to you, please seek help. You don't deserve to live with it for the rest of your life. It isn't your fault and you deserve so much better.

I have a great deal of compassion for my Mum, my Dad and my Grandpa. Writing this book has been instrumental in allowing me the time and space to think about them properly, to have empathy for them and to heal from my experience of the past. I would have loved to have got to this place while they were alive but I didn't and I will have to settle for thinking more kindly of them in their memory.

There are members of my birth family that I haven't written about in this book as this is my book and my story and it isn't my place to even begin to guess what their story is. My relationship is different with each one of them and we are all dealing with our experience of the past. I wish them nothing but love and I hope they too find some peace.

To you lovely reader, I hope you have enjoyed reading my story and if you can resonate with any part of my story I hope it brings you comfort to know you're not alone. You are special, you are enough and you too deserve a life that makes your heart and soul sing.

That is what I wish for you, for everyone.

It is hard knowing how to end this book after such an emotional rollercoaster writing it. I am a late comer to a lot of things, and I have written about some of them here, and I was also a late comer to watching the film, *The Greatest Showman*. I was deep in my therapy when I finally saw it and when I heard one of the songs the tears just wouldn't stop. It still moves me to tears every time I hear it. It feels like it's speaking to the core of me. The song is *This is Me* (written by Benj Pasek and Justin Paul, performed by Keala Settle, from The Greatest Showman soundtrack from Atlantic Records) and here are some of the lyrics that move me so deeply:

When the sharpest words wanna cut me down
I'm gonna send a flood, gonna drown 'em out
I am brave, I am bruised
I am who I'm meant to be, this is me
Look out 'cause here I come
And I'm marching on to the beat I drum

I'm not scared to be seen
I make no apologies, this is me

Freedom

The wind in my hair and on my face,
gently brushing my bare arms.
The sound of the waves calms me, makes
me smile.
The salt on my tongue is a joy to taste.
It has been too long.

The water rises and falls,
white foam covers my toes.
It is calling me in and I hear the call.
It is what I want to hear.
I'm in, I'm there, I'm beyond the breakers.

My boys are here too, we laugh out loud
together.
Like a mama whale with her calves.
We breech, we jump, we play.
The release, the relief, the wonder.
I can barely believe it is true.

My heart is beating the drum of life, this is
living, this is joy.
I have not stood alone this time while others
play.
I am doing what I want with people I love.
No judgement, no fear, no mean voice in my

head.
Freedom. At last.

Acknowledgements

I barely have the words to express my deep gratitude to my fabulous book coach, Sam Osbiston, who encouraged me to write this memoir rather than a self-help book. She saw the power and strength in what I wanted to say and supported me all the way. This book would not have been what it is without her.

The outstanding book cover is the work of Gary Bristow. Maxine Spring came up with an original concept that Gary took, along with my garbled ideas, and turned them into something just right.

All my early readers helped me shape the final version of this book. Their positivity and the way they accepted my book helped me have courage in the final push to publish it and put it out into the world. In no particular order, thank you to Diane Wensley, Lizzy House, Ewa Tuckett, Nick Tuckett, Chris Hochleitner, Luisa Tilocca, David Cooper, Jue Patricolo, Amanda Merbis-Kirk, Claire Holden, Sam Hardy, Dani Hill, Charlotte Squire-Davies, Rob Smith, Emma Hatherall, Chris Whitcombe,

Erin McCarthy.

To my husband Mark, thank you for the safe space to write this book from. To my boys, thank you for being you. To all my friends and family who have supported me over the last 12 months, thank you for being there for me.

I always knew that I wanted my book cover to be teal. It's my favourite colour. Teal is not green nor blue but a mix and shows that something beautiful is made when you bring the right things together. So my final thank you is to my Mum and my Dad for giving me life.

Information Sources:

For further information and support about the issues raised in this book, you can go to:

Children of Alcoholics – Nacoa (nacoa.org.uk)
Disordered eating – BEAT (beateatingdisorders.org.uk)
Grief – Cruse (cruse.org.uk)
General mental health support – Mind (mind.org.uk)
Counselling – to find a counsellor BACP (bacp.co.uk) and NCS (nationalcounsellingsociety.org)
Coaching – to find a life coach (lifecoach-directory.org.uk)

More about Philippa:

Philippa Robinson is a proud Northerner, who studied law at university, and she spent most of her career exploring the UK, subconsciously seeking "home". She settled in the beautiful city of Bristol where she now lives with her husband, two teenage sons and Bob the dog.

During her own personal transformation, through healing childhood trauma and learning to love and live for herself, she arrived at her soul mission to guide people to be the truest versions of themselves because she believes that is the greatest gift we can give ourselves. She proudly supports and volunteers with Nacoa (the National Association for Children of Alcoholics). Discovering a joy for writing, wild-swimming and even running (slowly) in mid-life has been a fabulous surprise.

Visit her website safeandsupported.co.uk where you can sign up for her newsletter, read her blog, listen to her podcast and check out her coaching packages. You will also find a gallery of the pictures referred to in this book.

Her podcast, Meeting of Minds, is available on Spotify, Google Podcasts, Apple Podcasts and all the usual platforms. You will find more of her story and her healing journey in the podcast episodes.

Follow her on Instagram (@safeandsupportedcoaching)

The best place to get in touch with Philippa is via the contact button on her website.

Printed in Great Britain
by Amazon

71539903R00213